To Beaver,
On the day of your

With love and prayers,

Rachel

30th May 1979.

Psalm 31 v 19.

Dictionary of Bible Words

John Eddison

Dictionary
of Bible Words

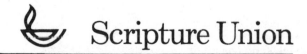 Scripture Union

© 1977 by John Eddison

First published 1977 by
Scripture Union, 47 Marylebone Lane,
London W1M 6AX

ISBN 0 85421 539 5

By the same author:

To Tell You the Truth
God's Frontiers
It's a Great Life
Christian Answers about Doctrine
Who Died Why
The Troubled Mind
What Makes a Leader?

Printed in Great Britain by
Billing & Sons Limited
Guildford, London and Worcester.

1. In compiling this reference book of Bible Words, three versions of the Bible have been used — Authorised (AV), Revised Standard (RSV) and New English (NEB).

2. Where these versions differ in their translation of a particular word, the most appropriate rendering has been chosen, the alternatives leading to it by means of a cross reference. Thus, for example, the word 'Earnest' (AV) = 'Pledge' (NEB) has been studied under 'Guarantee' (RSV); and 'Expiation' (RSV, NEB) under 'Propitiation' (AV).

3. In the commentary itself, reference to a particular version (AV, RSV, NEB) is only made when that version is definitely preferred to the others; and when the Bible itself is quoted, the version is only indicated if the quotation is fairly full or markedly different from the others.

4. Sometimes a word is not studied under its own name, but under another and more inclusive word. Thus, for example, there is a cross-reference from 'Doubt' to 'Unbelief', and from 'Trespass' to 'Sin'.

5. A few words (e.g. 'Incarnation', 'Trinity') have been included although they do not actually occur in the Bible. This is because the Bible itself did not coin a word for some scriptural truths or concepts, and it was only later on that a suitable one was evolved.

To the other members of
'PECKAM'
whose friendship and encouragement
have meant so much to me.

Abba

This is the Aramaic word for 'Father', from which our word 'Abbot' is derived. It is used by Jesus himself in prayer in a very personal way (Mark 14:36), and later by Christians as well (Romans 8:15. Galatians 4:6). The word had a less formal meaning than 'Father' and could fairly be translated as 'Dad'. In most of our English versions the word appears in its original form, perhaps to avoid what might appear as familiarity with God, but more likely because it preserved a primitive expression which had become very precious to the Aramaic-speaking Christian Church.

Accept

1. Man, being sinful, cannot be received or welcomed by a holy God on the grounds of his own merits or achievements. His acceptance depends upon what Christ has done for him (Ephesians 1:6,7 AV) and is freely bestowed as a favour.
2. It follows that what man offers to God is only acceptable if he himself is in a right relationship with God (Hosea 8:13. Malachi 1:10,13). This is why Cain's sacrifice was not accepted (Hebrews 11:4), and it applies to our prayers (Acts 10:4), worship (Hebrews 12:28 RSV) and service (Romans 12:1,2).

Access

This is a nautical word in the Greek, meaning a 'landing-stage', and in Romans 5:2 AV 'access ... into this grace' probably contains the idea of an approach into a harbour; and it is also used to describe an approach for an audience with a king.

In Old Testament days God's presence within 'the Holy of Holies' was protected by a veil or curtain, beyond which only the High Priest could venture once a year, after making the appropriate sacrifice (Hebrews 9:1-10). Through his death, Jesus gained 'the right of way', the access into God's immediate presence for all those who believe in him (Hebrews 10:19-22. Romans 5:2. Ephesians 2:18. 1 Peter 3:18); and the opening of this 'new and living way' was symbolized at the time of his death by the rending of the curtain in the temple at Jerusalem (Matthew 27:51).

Adoption
(See CHILDREN OF GOD)

Adultery

The literal meaning of this word is of course obvious, and covers all forms of marital unfaithfulness which are condemned throughout the Bible (Exodus 20:14), while Jesus showed that the sin consisted not only in the act, but in the lustful thoughts which led up to it (Matthew 5:27,28).

But the word is a popular metaphor of the Old Testament prophets to describe the unfaithfulness of God's people to him, and their readiness to desert him for idols of wood and stone (Jeremiah 3:8,9. Ezekiel 23:37). It may have been with this in mind that Jesus referred to the Jews of his day as 'an evil and adulterous generation' (Matthew 12:39), because they would not believe his word or turn to him.

Advocate

(See also COUNSELLOR)
This is the word preferred by the NEB for 'Comforter' (AV) and 'Counsellor' (RSV) and used in John's Gospel to describe the Holy Spirit (see article). There is however one place where all three versions use the word (1 John 2:1) and there it refers not to the Holy Spirit, but to Christ. It pictures him as our legal counsellor or advocate ('advocatus' — 'called alongside'), pleading our cause in God's presence, and claiming forgiveness for us on the ground of his own death upon the cross.

Ambassador

The Greek word translated 'Ambassador' in the AV, RSV and NEB is really a verb 'to ambassadorise', and is closely related to the word translated elsewhere in the New Testament as 'elder'. It was used of a senior citizen who might be on an embassy to the Emperor. It only occurs twice in the New Testament — in 2 Corinthians 5:20 and in Ephesians 6:20, where Paul speaks of himself as an 'ambassador in chains'.

The ambassador is a *representative* of Jesus Christ, and also a *messenger* who tries to bring about 'reconciliation' between the people to whom he is sent and the King he represents (2 Corinthians 5:20). But the connexion between ambassador and king is so close, that the ambassador is really only a channel or vehicle for passing on what the king has to say. The message and the authority behind it are derived from the king himself. It must follow too that the ambassador is also a *foreigner*, who cannot always expect to be accepted and understood (John 15:18-20).

Amen

This word means 'verily', 'truly' or 'indeed', and coming at the end of sentences may be translated 'so let it be'. The root idea of the word is 'trustworthiness', and in Old Testament times it became the formal way of accepting an oath or a curse (Deuteronomy 27:15) or a prophecy (Jeremiah 28:6 AV, RSV), as well as an expression of agreement with prayer or praise (1 Chronicles 16:36. Psalm 41:13).

Christ frequently introduced his teaching with the double use of the word ('Truly, truly ...' John 1:51 RSV), as though to emphasise its authority and truth. It was applied by Paul to the promises of God (2 Corinthians 1:20), and finally as a name for Christ himself ('The Amen' — Revelation 3:14). This affirmed the fact that he is indeed the 'God of truth' (Isaiah 65:16), or as the NEB puts it: 'the God whose name is Amen'.

Angel

The Greek word *angelos* really means 'messenger', and is translated in this way in the New Testament when it refers to an ordinary human being (Luke 7:24); but more usually it refers to a quite separately created order of heavenly beings.

Their nature. There is nothing in the Bible to suggest that they are human beings who have been elevated to a kind of spiritual peerage, but rather that they are spiritual beings (Hebrews 1:7) who

11

have been specially created for particular tasks before the creation of the world (Job 38.7). They appear to be endowed with free will, and it seems clear from some parts of the Bible that Satan himself once belonged to this order, and used his privileged position to rebel, along with others, against God (Job 4:18 AV, RSV. Isaiah 14:12-17. Matthew 25:41. 2 Peter 2:4. Revelation 12:9).

Their task. Their first task was to act almost as courtiers in God's heavenly palace, guarding the way into his presence (Genesis 3:24), attending him (Isaiah 6:1-4) and perhaps even sharing with him in the great work of creation (Job 38:7), law-giving (Acts 7:53. Galatians 3:19. Hebrews 2:2) and final judgement (Matthew 16:27. 2 Thessalonians 1:7-10).

The second function of angels was to act as God's agents for the benefit of mankind, sometimes bringing more practical assistance: and the expression 'Guardian Angel' describes the watchful care which they exercise over God's people (Matthew 18:10. Hebrews 1:13,14). It was an angel, for example, who came to Hagar's assistance (Genesis 16:7-14), sustained Elijah after his great ordeal on Mount Carmel (1 Kings 19:1-8), warned Joseph to escape into Egypt (Matthew 2:13), came to the rescue of Peter (Acts 12:7) and stood by Paul at some of the most critical moments of his life (Acts 27:23). It is interesting to notice too that Jesus, who although he was superior to the angels (Hebrews 1) and had been made lower than they for the suffering of death (Hebrews 2:9), was himself the object of their care and attention. They were particularly in evidence at his birth (Luke 2:8-14), his temptation (Matthew 4:11), his agony in the garden (Luke 22:43) and his resurrection (Matthew 28:1-8).

Their form. We are told little of what angels looked like, although references to their countenance and their clothing (Matthew 28:2,3. Luke 2:9. Acts 1:10) suggest a kind of majestic beauty which may have reflected itself in the face of the martyr Stephen (Acts 6:15). Nor does there seem to have been any fixed pattern with regard to their appearances. There were occasions when God himself was revealed to people in angelic form (Genesis 18. Joshua 5:13-15), or when the being was clearly some kind of visitor from another world (Matthew 28:2); while at other times they seem to have been indistinguishable from ordinary people (Genesis 19:1-3. Hebrews 13:2), or to have made themselves known simply by a voice (Genesis 22:11).

12

Anger

In the normal way, as applied to human beings, anger is regarded in the Bible as something to be 'put away', like malice and blasphemy (Ephesians 4:31. Colossians 3:8); but the Bible does recognize the fact that there is such a thing as 'righteous indignation', that sometimes it can have a good cause and that it is not to be automatically equated with sin. In one place Paul actually says, 'If you are angry, do not let anger lead you into sin' (Ephesians 4:26 NEB).

In Scripture God's attitude towards sin is described in the terms of human passion. He is angry with the wicked (Psalm 7:11), wrathful when his people disobey him (Exodus 32:10) and indignant with those who oppose him (Malachi 1:4. Mark 10:14). The language does not express irrational action by God, but describes the settled and permanent attitude of someone who is holy and just towards wickedness in every shape and form. There is nothing capricious or temperamental about God's anger. He is never irritated. He is, as Augustine says, 'angry, without being the least disturbed'. At the same time it would be a mistake to think of his anger as simply an automatic and inevitable reaction — rather as we speak of justice 'taking its course'. It has a personal quality about it, for sin is not only the breaking of God's law, it is also the rejection of his sovereignty and his love.

We find in the Bible, particularly in the Old Testament, a number of occasions on which the wrath of God was displayed against people and against cities — Sodom and Gomorrah (Deuteronomy 29:23), for example, and Nineveh (Nahum 1:2-6); but it will only be fully and finally unfolded at the day of judgement (Revelation 6:16,17), which is sometimes referred to as 'the day of his wrath' ('Dies irae').

Anointing

This was an Old Testament practice whereby objects and people were smeared with holy oil, and set apart for a special purpose. The tabernacle and its furniture (Exodus 30:22-33), for example, were treated in this way; while it was the custom to consecrate Kings (2 Samuel 2:4), Prophets (1 Kings 19:16) and Priests (Exodus 28:41) to their sacred office in the same manner.

The Jews looked forward eagerly to the coming of their 'Messiah' (Greek: *christos*) which means 'the Anointed One', and they expected him to combine within himself these three offices of

13

prophet, priest and king. When Jesus claimed to be the Messiah (John 4:25,26), it meant that he had done precisely this. He had come into the world as the perfect Prophet (to proclaim God's Word), Priest (to offer 'a full, perfect and sufficient sacrifice for the sins of the whole world') and King (to establish the Kingdom of God).

Oil, when used in consecration, is a symbol of the Holy Spirit (1 Samuel 16:13. Isaiah 61:1), and in the New Testament we find that it is he who came upon Jesus at his baptism, equipping him for his work (Mark 1:9-11. Luke 4:18. Acts 4:27). It was he who anointed the disciples on the Day of Pentecost (Acts 2:1-4); and it was he again who endowed the early Christians with spiritual knowledge and understanding (1 John 2:20,27) and power (Acts 4:8; 13:9). Instances of anointing with oil in the New Testament refer either to the practice of welcoming a guest (Luke 7:46), healing the sick (Mark 6:13. Luke 10:34. James 5:14), or embalming the dead (Mark 14:8; 16:1). The healing properties of oil, whether applied externally or taken internally, were well known; but from some New Testament references (eg James 5:14) it appears that it may have acquired a sacramental as well as a medicinal value.

Apostasy

This word means a 'withdrawal' or 'desertion'. It is rarely if ever used except in a religious context, though it could fairly be applied, for example, to someone who had forsaken his political party for another one. It occurs only twice in the New Testament (Acts 21:21. 2 Thessalonians 2:3) and is translated variously in different versions as 'forsaking', 'falling away' or 'rebellion'. It is related to the Greek word for 'divorce', and this idea underlines the reference to 'apostate Israel' (Jeremiah 3:8 NEB), where the country is compared to 'that faithless woman, her sister, Judah', because they have proved faithless and dealt treacherously with the living God who wanted them for himself alone.

The word implies the desertion of a stand once taken rather than the original rejection of God's claims, and throughout the Bible his people are warned of the peculiar dangers of this particular sin. Christians must realize that there are many false teachers about who would seduce them from the purity of the truth (Matthew 24:11. Galatians 1:6-8; 2:4. 2 Peter 2:1,2); that apostasy seems to be one of the marks of 'the latter times' (1 Timothy 4:1-4); and that a point can be reached at which it is impossible for the apostate to be renewed to his former state (Hebrews 6:4-6; 10:26), for he has

14

committed the 'deadly sin' (1 John 5:16 NEB) which has seemingly put him even beyond the reach of prayer.

Apostle
This word was used to describe those who had been 'sent out' with the message of Christ (Greek 'apostello': 'I send'). In one sense therefore it included a much wider circle than The Twelve (Acts 14:4,14. Romans 16:7), but it was usually applied more narrowly to those who had received a personal commission from the Lord whom they had actually seen.

It was this qualification which was carefully emphasised when the Eleven were trying to find a successor to Judas (Acts 1:21-26); and when Paul's apostleship was challenged (2 Corinthians 11:5-13), he defended his claim to it on the grounds that he too had seen the risen Christ and had received a personal commission from him (Acts 9:1-9. 1 Corinthians 15:8-10. Galatians 1:1; 11-17).

But the apostles were not only messengers and witnesses, they were also the depository and interpreters of Christian doctrine (Acts 2:42 AV, RSV. cf 1 John 2:19), and in this sense, together with the 'prophets', they are described as 'the foundation' of the Christian Church (Ephesians 2:20).

Strictly speaking therefore there are no apostles today, and what is called 'the apostolic age' ended with the death of the first generation of Christians; but the apostolic message has been permanently enshrined in the New Testament, and the apostolic work is carried on by successive generations of Christian men and women.

Ascension
The account of the Ascension of Jesus Christ into heaven is found in two places —Luke 24:51 and Acts 1:4-11. He himself spoke of it when he was on earth (John 6:62), and referred at other times to the fact that he would be returning to his Father (John 14:1-4).

It is sometimes argued that the Ascension cannot have taken place as described, because it assumes an out-dated idea of heaven as a place 'up there'. But the following points are worth noting.

1. Jesus was trying to show simple people, not twentieth-century scientists, that he was making a final and miraculous departure from earth, and the most obvious way to do it was to go 'up'. It is difficult to think of any other mode of departure which would have been as convincing or would not have led to even more difficult questions.

2. If the word 'heaven' means anything at all, it must be somewhere away from this earth, outside the space-time framework in which we live. To think of it therefore as being upwards is perfectly reasonable and logical, and was the way in which Jesus had taught his disciples to imagine it (John 17:1).

3. The whole idea of 'going up' suggests promotion to a higher state. It is a symbol of glory, just as 'coming down' was a symbol of grace; and we can be sure that this was not lost upon those who were present or heard about it afterwards. We are told that Christ is now seated at God's right hand (Hebrews 1:3). This suggests that he is resting from a completed work (John 19:30. Hebrews 10:12), that he has been given a place of honour, and that his nearness to the Father guarantees that we are accepted by God (1 John 2:1,2) and that our prayers are heard (Hebrews 7:25). It is here, where he has entered as our forerunner (Hebrews 8:1; 9:24; 12:2), that his effective Lordship begins (Acts 2:36) and where he awaits his ultimate victory (Acts 3:21. Philippians 2:9-11).

Assurance

The Bible indicates two kinds of assurance — historical and experimental.

1. *Historical.* The foundation of the Christian's faith is not a philosophy or system of thought, but events which actually took place in history (2 Peter 1:16), namely, the birth, life, death and resurrection of Jesus Christ; and it was the last of these which provided the crowning proof that he was what he claimed to be—the Son of God (Romans 1:4).

2. *Experimental.* To match these objective historical facts the Christian believer also has what the Bible calls 'the witness in himself' (1 John 5:10 AV). This is the work of the Holy Spirit convincing him beyond any shadow of doubt that he is a child of God (Romans 8:16). It is in this assurance that he can come to God in prayer (Hebrews 10:22), testify to the truth of the gospel (1 Thessalonians 1:5) and look forward to the final hope to be with Christ (Hebrews 6:11 AV, RSV).

But it must not be supposed that this inner conviction exists only in the realm of feelings. It has practical outworkings, as John is careful to show in his epistles. The true child of God practises righteousness and not sin (1 John 2:29; 3:9), overcomes the temptations in the world (1 John 4:4; 5:4) and loves his fellow-Christians (1 John 4:7).

16

Atonement
(See PROPITIATION)

Authority
This word is of chief interest and importance in its New Testament application to Christ. Although he refused to tell his critics from where his authority came, he made it quite clear on a number of other occasions that it was derived direct from God himself (John 17:2. Matthew 28:18), the one and only source of all authority and power (Psalm 93:1,2).

Jesus revealed his authority in a number of ways. It was seen in *his teaching*, and it was this which distinguished him in the minds of the ordinary people from the religious leaders of the day (Mark 1:22); for 'they were astounded at his teaching, for what he said had the note of authority' (Luke 4:32 NEB). He showed it in the way *he forgave* people their sins (Mark 2:5-7), and this in the eyes of his enemies was the ultimate blasphemy, because to claim to forgive sins was to make himself equal with God. The same authority was seen in *his miracles* (Mark 1:27,28), in the way in which he *controlled the programme* of his life (John 10:17,18), and in the fact that God committed to him *the judgement of mankind* (John 5:27. Acts 17:31).

But we must also notice that the authority of Christ was delegated in the first instance to his followers (Luke 9:1; 10:17. Matthew 28:20). It was in his name and with his authority that they went into the world to preach the gospel (Acts 1:8), acting as his ambassadors (2 Corinthians 5:20); to build up and regulate his Church (2 Corinthians 10:8); to appoint church leaders (Acts 6:3); to lay down guide-lines concerning faith and conduct (2 Thessalonians 2:15; 3:4,6,14). In doing all these things they rested on the commission they had received from Christ himself (John 20:21), and believed that their own commands and advice had the stamp of his divine authority (1 Corinthians 14:37).

Finally this authority was invested in the Scriptures; for the Old Testament looks forward to his coming (John 5:39), while the New Testament looks back on his life and ministry and sees it as the pattern and yardstick of Christian belief and practice (2 Timothy 3:16); and it is for this reason that we often speak of the Scriptures as 'the Word of God' (Romans 10:17 AV).

17

B

Baptism

The popular use of the word suggests 'initiation' into something. The soldier, for example, has his 'baptism of fire'. But the Greek word really means to 'dip or submerge', usually in a ceremonial sense, and the rite was practised in pre-Christian days in some Jewish sects to signify repentance and forgiveness of sins. It was for this purpose that John the Baptist administered the rite (Mark 1:4), those submitting to it showing their determination to abandon their sins and allow them to be washed away. Jesus did nothing to destroy this original idea, but baptism gradually acquired a deeper significance as it was taken over into Christian thinking later in the New Testament.

1. It was closely associated with the work of the Holy Spirit (Matthew 3:11. Acts 1:5; 11:16, &c), because it was realized that it was he alone who could bring conviction of sin (John 16:7-9) and produce a work of repentance and faith in the hearts of people.
2. It also became associated with the death and resurrection of Jesus, the candidate being 'buried with him in baptism' and then 'raised with him through faith' (Colossians 2:12. Romans 6:3,4).
3. It became the New Testament counterpart of circumcision, that is to say, the outward and visible sign of a new covenant relationship with God.

18

4. It was a way of signifying personal identity with Christ and membership of God's family, and as such it was considered a necessary and immediate sequel to conversion (Matthew 28:19. Acts 2:38,41; 8:36-38; 9:18, &c).

5. Those who baptize the children of Christian families after the pattern of infant circumcision (Genesis 17:11), believe that the households who were baptized included children (Acts 16:33. 1 Corinthians 1:16).

6. No rules are given for the method of baptism. Baptism as burial with Christ (Romans 6:4) would be symbolized by immersion. Baptism as putting on Christ (Galatians 3:27) would be symbolized by pouring on the water, just as the baptism by the Spirit at Pentecost (Acts 1:5) was the pouring out of the Spirit upon the disciples (Acts 2:17).

(See also CIRCUMCISION)

Bishop

The word really means 'overseer' or 'supervisor' or 'guardian' and was used in the New Testament to describe a senior member of the local Christian Church. It is virtually interchangeable with another word translated 'elder' in many parts of the New Testament, as may be seen by comparing Acts 20:17 with Acts 20:28, though 'elder' had a Jewish and 'overseer' a Greek origin.

It seems therefore that in the local churches of the New Testament period there were only two officers — deacons and elders (overseers). The deacons were largely concerned with administration (Acts 6:1-6), leaving the elders free to take a more active spiritual lead; but here again the division was not hard and fast, and there is some overlapping in the qualifications required for each office (1 Timothy 3:1-13. Titus 1:7-9).

There is nothing in the New Testament to suggest what is sometimes called 'Monarchical Episcopacy', as practised in the Church of England today; but on the other hand it was probably a natural and inevitable development as the Church grew, and outstandingly gifted men became elected as permanent chairmen of the councils of Church elders; e.g. James at Jerusalem (Acts 15).

Blasphemy

To blaspheme is to speak against God, to insult him or in any way to slander or speak evil of him. In the Old Testament it was a sin which was punishable by death (Leviticus 24:10-14. See also Acts 6:11), and though it was usually confined to the heathen (Isaiah

19

37:23), the idolatry of God's own people amounted to almost the same thing (Romans 2:24). In the New Testament the meaning is sometimes extended to include slanderous utterances against God's representatives such as Moses (Acts 6:11), Paul (Romans 3:8) and Jesus (Matthew 27:39).

We must also consider here what is meant by the 'unforgivable sin' which is described as 'blasphemy against the Holy Spirit' (Mark 3:28-30). It is clear from the context that it refers to that state of mind which can attribute the works of Christ to the devil. It is totally insensitive towards right and wrong, and finally expresses itself in the words of Milton's Satan, 'Evil be thou my good' (cf Isaiah 5:18-20). It is obvious that forgiveness of this sin is impossible, because repentance is impossible to a person who seriously supposes that the evil he has done is good. It is in fact a persistent attitude, described as hardness of heart. Some introspective Christians have been concerned that some single sin they have committed may be the unforgivable sin. The fact that they are concerned is a sign that it is not unforgivable, so the Holy Spirit is convicting them with a view to repentance and forgiveness.

Blessed

In the Old Testament the word translated 'Bless' means 'Praise' when applied to God (Psalm 104:1) and 'Blessed' means 'Happy' when applied to man (Psalm 1:1). In the New Testament this distinction is kept, the Greek word *eulogetos* referring to God (Luke 1:68) and *makarios* to man (Matthew 5:5). Occasionally the role is reversed, *eulogetos* being applied to man, in which case 'favoured' is perhaps the best translation (Luke 1:28) and *makarios* to God, when the NEB renders it, 'God in his eternal felicity' (1 Timothy 1:11; 6:15).

Blessing

Throughout the Bible this word is used to indicate a favour, whether material (Deuteronomy 28:8) or spiritual (Ephesians 1:3) bestowed by one person (usually God himself) upon another. Sometimes the word is usee to describe the praise of God (James 3:9,10), and in one place (Romans 16:18) it is actually used to describe flattery (AV 'fair speeches').

Blood

In Leviticus 17:11 we read that 'the life of the flesh is in the blood',

20

and this phrase gives us the clue to the use of the word 'blood' throughout the Bible. It nearly always means 'a life laid down', and in fact we get near this idea in our own language when we speak of 'bloodshed', which has come to be used as almost an equivalent word for death.

It is because of this that the blood is regarded in the Bible with such sacred significance. In the Old Testament sacrifices the flesh of the animal was partly offered to God and partly consumed by the people, for the sharing of a meal was a mark of friendship and communion; but the drinking of the blood of the animal was strictly forbidden, and it had to be poured out upon the altar to remind the people that friendship and peace with God could only come through sacrifice (Leviticus 3 and 7).

Turning to the New Testament, we find that it is through the blood of Christ, or through the sacrifice of himself upon the cross, that the believer enjoys peace with God (Colossians 1:20), freedom from the slavery of sin (Revelation 1:5), cleansing from it defilement (1 John 1:7), redemption (1 Peter 1:18,19), forgiveness (Ephesians 1:7) and justification (Romans 5:9). The Old Testament animal sacrifices provided a limited remedy for sin, but the death of Christ obtained eternal salvation for us (Hebrews 9:11-14), because his death was infinitely more precious than theirs; for the blood of Christ was not only human, it was also divine (Acts 20:28 AV).

Not only was the blood the means whereby man entered a new relationship with God, but it was the visible sign or seal that a covenant between them had been established (Exodus 12 and 24. Matthew 26:28). It both created and confirmed the peace treaty between man and God.

Brotherly Love
(See LOVE)

Children of God

Apart from one or two occasions where it is used to describe supernaturally created beings (Genesis 6:1,2. Job 1:6), the phrase 'sons of God' applies to a special relationship between God and man. There is a sense in which all mankind is 'the offspring' of God (Acts 17:28,29), that is to say, of the same stock or kind (Genesis 1:26,27); and in the Old Testament Israel is said to be related to God in this particularly personal way (Deuteronomy 14:1. Hosea 11:1).

But it is in the New Testament that the phrase assumes its special importance, where it is used to describe those who have put their trust in Christ (John 1:12,13. Galatians 3:26), the rest of mankind being described as 'the children of the wicked one' (Matthew 13:38 AV. John 8:44. 1 John 3:8-10).

Two different metaphors are used in the New Testament to describe the nature of this relationship. John favours that of birth, or *regeneration,* the believer being 'born again' (John 3:5) into God's family and into a new life. This theme is strongly developed in his epistles, where the phrase 'born of God' constantly occurs (1 John 3:9; 4:7; 5:1. &c). Paul, on the other hand, although not excluding this metaphor (Titus 3:5), makes greater use of the idea of *adoption* from slavery to sonship (Romans 8:15. Galatians 4:1-5).

The two are complementary, and emphasise the richness of this relationship. John stresses its moral and spiritual aspect, and the development of a Christ-like nature which is pleasing to God; while Paul underlines the more legal aspect of our new standing with God as fellow-heirs with Christ (Romans 8:17), and the enjoyment of the inheritance we find in him (Ephesians 1:3-12).

Christian

This was the nickname by which the followers of Jesus became generally known, and which was applied to them for the first time at Antioch (Acts 11:26). The suffix *ianos* seems to have been a common way in Greek of expressing loyalty to a particular person. Thus we read of the 'Herodians' (Mark 3:6 — 'partisans of Herod' NEB), and therefore *Christianos* became a perfectly natural way of referring to the adherents of Christ. See also 1 Peter 4:16.

Church

There is a confusion here which we must try to clear up at the outset. Our English word 'church' comes from the Greek word *kuriakos* meaning 'the Lord's', later used in a phrase like *kuriakon doma*, 'the Lord's house', referring to a building where the local congregation of Christians met. Similarly *kuriake hemera*, 'the Lord's Day' (Revelation 1:10).

But the word translated 'church' in the New Testament is *ekklesia*, which comes from a verb meaning 'to call out', and is used to describe a local assembly of Christians and never a building. The word is not peculiar to the New Testament, and was also used in other contexts to describe a gathering of people met for a particular purpose; but in the New Testament it refers to those who have responded to the call of Christ, and have been formed into a fellowship for the purpose of prayer and worship. The aggregate of such fellowships became known as 'the Church', the body of believers everywhere. (e.g. Matthew 16:18; 1 Timothy 3:15). The New Testament is rich in metaphors which describe the nature of the Church. It is compared to a *building* (Ephesians 2:19-22), founded upon the apostles and prophets, with Christ himself as the chief corner stone, consecrated to the service of God, and indwelt by the Holy Spirit, just as individual Christians are (1 Corinthians 3:10-17); to a *body* (Ephesians 4:16) in which each part makes its particular contribution to the welfare of the whole (1 Corinthians

12:12); and to a *bride* (Ephesians 5:23-27), belonging exclusively to Christ himself.

The function of the Christian Church is nowhere more clearly set out than in 1 Peter 2:1-10, where we see that its task is to 'offer up' (5) and to 'show forth' (9). The Godward function of the Church is to offer to him the sacrifices of prayer, praise and thanksgiving; while its manward function is to show forth or display the virtues and excellencies of God. In other words, the twofold function of the Church is to worship and to witness.

Circumcision

Circumcision was the outward and physical sign in the flesh of the male Israelite of the special relationship enjoyed by the Children of Israel with God, and was the proof of the covenant which existed between them (Genesis 17:10-14).

In the New Testament there was some controversy as to what part if any circumcision should play, and Paul laid down three main principles. First, he insisted that the Jews could not expect the outward sign to bring them any special advantage if the inward grace was missing (Romans 2:25-29). Secondly, it was quite unnecessary for Gentile Christians to undergo this rite before they could enjoy the full benefits of the new covenant with Christ (Galatians 6:11-14), of which baptism and not circumcision was to be the sign. Thirdly, what really counts is what Paul called the 'circumcision of the heart' (Romans 2:29. Colossians 2:11), that is to say, the putting away or cutting out of the Christian's life all that is sinful and displeasing to God.

Some Christians have seen in this rite, which was performed in infancy, a justification for the baptism of the children of Christian parents before they are old enough to make a conscious profession of faith; while others, though admitting the value of some sort of ceremony of initiation for the children of Christian parents, have felt that this should not be baptism, on the grounds that this rite should always follow a profession of personal faith. (See Baptism).

Comforter

(See COUNSELLOR)

Commandments

(See also LAW)

This word is used throughout the Bible to describe the precepts by which God wants to order the lives of his creatures. We find it in

24

use (Genesis 26:5) well before that special code of conduct was given through Moses which we know as the 'Ten Commandments' (Exodus 20), and nor is it later confined to them.

In the New Testament we find that Jesus did two things to the Old Testament commandments. First, he amplified them, giving them a new and deeper meaning, in fact another dimension. He did this by showing that they did not simply apply to outward actions, but also to the words and thoughts which give rise to such actions (Matthew 5:21,22; 27,28). He 'fulfilled' them in the sense that one might fill in the bare outline of a map with rivers, mountains and roads, giving it content and substance.

Secondly, he simplified them by reducing them from ten to two (Mark 12:28-34). In doing so, however, he was not making love a substitute for the Commandments, but rather showing that there was no commandment which could be broken without offending at some point against the principle of love (Romans 13:10). Perfect love means perfect obedience (John 14:15).

Communion
(See FELLOWSHIP)

Condemnation
(See JUDGEMENT)

Confession
The same word is used throughout the Bible in two distinct senses.

1. It means to acknowledge our sins before God, which in Old Testament and New Testament alike is regarded as the first condition of forgiveness (Psalm 32:5. Proverbs 28:13. Matthew 3:6. 1 John 1:9). This involves coming to God in the humble, penitent spirit of the prodigal son (Luke 15:18) and the publican (Luke 18:13), and asking for his pardon.

2. It is also the word used of Christian witness, as we acknowledge openly before others our faith in Christ (Matthew 10:32, AV. Romans 10:9,10). We are told too that there will come a time when mankind as a whole will be brought to the place of public admission 'that Jesus Christ is Lord' (Philippians 2:9-11).

Confirm
As used in the New Testament, this word has no connexion with the rite of Confirmation as practised in the Church of England, which traces its origin to quite different sources. The three Greek words are non-technical words, and simply mean to make firm or

to establish. They are applied to God's word and promises (Hebrews 2:3. Romans 15:8) and to individual Christian people (Acts 14:22). Modern translations normally use equivalent words like 'sustain' or 'strengthen'.

Conscience

The Bible nowhere defines conscience, but rather takes it for granted that everyone knows what it is from personal experience. The Greek word means 'co-knowledge', or that inner echo which corresponds with what we know from external and objective standards to be right and wrong. In the case of the Jew, this standard was the Law; while for the Gentile it was the character of God revealed to him in the natural order of things (Romans 2:12-16). The word itself hardly occurs in the Old Testament, but the idea is found, for example, in 1 Samuel 24:5 AV, RSV, where we reed that 'David's heart (NEB 'conscience') smote him' over his treatment of Saul. In the New Testament it plays an important part in the eching of Paul. It is the conscience to which the gospel appeals (2 Corinthians 4:2), because it recognizes the truth of what is being said, and it is conscience which like a rudder guides theiourse of a Christian's conduct(1 Timothy 1:19). However, it is possible for the conscience to become so damaged and distorted (1 Timothy 4:2. Titus 1:15) that it will no longer act as a reliable barometer of good and evil.

The Christian will do all he can to keep a clear conscience (Acts 23:1; 24:16. 1 Timothy 1:5), testing it always by the standard of God's Word, and relying upon it increasingly as an accurate moral indicator (Romans 9:1; 13:5). But he will go even further than this, for he will find sometimes that his own behaviour will be inspired, not by his own consciece, however enlightened it may be, but by that of a weaker Christian (1 Corinthians 8), and that he will refrain from what he himself considers to be harmless for the sake of an immature Christian who considers it to be wrong.

Consecration

(See SANCTIFICATION)

Conversation

The AV uses this word as an equivalent for 'behaviour', 'manner of life', 'conduct' or 'habits', and these much more accurate translatons are preferred in modern translations (See Galatians 1:13. 1 Timothy 4:12 &c). There is also one place in the AV

(Philippians 3:20) where a different Greek word is rendered 'conversation', and here the correct translation is 'citizenship', which is to be found in more modern versions.

Conversion

Although in common use in Christian circles, the word Conversion is used once only in the AV (Acts 15:3). The corresponding verb, both in Hebrew and Greek occurs several times (e.g. Psalm 51:13. Acts 3:19) where modern translations commonly bring out the meaning with 'turn back', or 'return'. Such an action obviously implies the turning from an old way of life and a turning towards Christ (Acts 14:15; 26:18. 1 Thessalonians 1:9). The first involves a change of heart and mind, and the second a personal trust in Jesus Christ; and these two repentance and faith (Acts 20:21) together constitute true conversion. Conversion is the way we enter the Kingdom of God (Matthew 18:3), and begin to enjoy in our own experience the benefits of Christ's death and resurrection; his forgiveness, friendship and power (Acts 3:19; 26:18). Nowhere pehaps in the whole Bible is the meaning of Conversion more clearly and vividly expressed than in Isaiah 55:6,7.
(See also REGENERATION)

Counsellor

(See also HOLY SPIRIT)
This is the word used in the RSV instead of 'Comforter' (AV) and 'Advocate' (NEB) to describe the person and work of the Holy Spirit in John's Gospel (John 14:16,26; 15:26; 16:7). All three words are attempts to translate the Greek word *Parakletos,* which in its active sense means 'an encourager' or 'consoler', while passively it means 'someone called alongside to help' (Latin: *advocatus*). Matthew 10:19,20 gives us a picture of him at work, encouraging, consoling, advising the Christian believer.
The word 'Advocate' (see article) suggests a Counsellor in a legal sense, and this idea may be present in John 16:7-11, although in this case, where unbelievers are concerned, the Holy Spirit seems to be acting as 'Counsel for the Prosecution'.

Covenant

A 'covenant' or 'testament' in the Bible is different from a treaty or pact between people or countries, when both parties agree to certain conditions, because it is a unilateral, sovereign act on the part of God, who imposes what conditions he chooses. In some respects it is more like a will (Hebrews 9:16,17), in which the testator makes his bequests exactly as he chooses, and they cannot be altered by anyone else.

In the Old Testament there are several personal covenants. There is one with Noah (Genesis 9:9-17), when God promised that the earth would not again be flooded; with Abraham, from whose family a great nation would grow (Genesis 17:6-8); with Moses, to whom God promised that he would adopt his people Israel (Deuteronomy 7:6-11); and with David (Psalm 89:3,4, 26-37), from whose line would one day come the promised Messiah. In all these covenants the two most important features were the faithfulness of God and the required holiness of man.

The 'New Testament', like the 'Old', was the result of God's initiative and grace. On God's part the offer was one of the total 'remission (or forgiveness) of their sins' (Luke 1:77), while on man's part there must be repentance and faith (Acts 20:21). But this Covenant differed in three ways from some of those that had gone before. It was universal in its application, and not just to one family, tribe or nation (1 John 2:2); it was everlasting, and could never be cancelled (Hebrews 13:20); and, unlike some of the others, it was faultless (Hebrews 8:7). Finally, we notice that the price and the pledge of this New Covenant was the blood of Jesus Christ himself (Matthew 26:28. Hebrews 10:29).

Covetousness

I am not being covetous if I like and admire another person's garden or furniture, but only when I begin to desire to extend my influence over those things and possess them for myself. This is what is expressly forbidden in the Tenth Commandment (Exodus 20:17). It is forbidden partly no doubt because it is wrong in itself, and partly because of the other sins it can often lead to, such as theft (Joshua 7:16-26), adultery (2 Samuel 11) and murder (Mark 14:10,11).

The New Testament uses two Greek words to translate this idea of covetousness.

1. *Epithumia* describes any strong desire or passion, and though the word can be used neutrally and even in a good sense (Hebrews 6:11. 1 Peter 1:12), the overtones are normally unfavourable (Matthew 5:28. Acts 20:33), and it is intended to convey the idea of

misdirected desires. The word is translated in different ways in the various versions — 'lust', 'desire', 'want'.

2. *Pleonexia* is a stronger and more unfavourable word, and includes an entire disregard for the rights and interests of others in seeking what it desires for itself. It is normally translated 'covetousness' in the AV (Luke 12:15. But 'greediness' in Ephesians 4:19); though perhaps the NEB gets nearest the true meaning of the word when it renders it 'rapacity' (Romans 1:29) and 'ruthless greed' (Ephesians 5:3).

Creation (Creator)

In several places in the Bible the title Creator is applied directly to God (Isaiah 40:28. Ecclesiastes 12:1. Romans 1:25. &c); while in many others his creative work is described (Isaiah 40:26; 42:5; 45:18. Psalm 104:5. &c). It is at his command (Psalm 33:6,9) and through his sovereign power (Jeremiah 10:11-13) that the universe and all that is in it were made from nothing (Genesis 1:1); and this is something which Christians have always accepted, not only because it seems to them reasonable and logical to do so, but 'through faith' (Hebrews 11:3).

The early chapters of Genesis do not set out to give an exact and scientific account of how things came to exist, but rather they give a poetical and yet ordered description of the appearance of all natural phenomena, by the creative will of God, culminating in that of man himself (Genesis 1:26-28).

The work of Creation is attributed to all three persons of the Trinity. Not only is it the work of the Father, as we have seen, but the Bible also associates the Son with this creative work (John 1:3,10. Colossians 1:16. Hebrews 1:1,2), and the Holy Spirit (Genesis 1:2. Job 33:4).

When we seek a purpose in the Bible for Creation, it is probably not necessary to look beyond Genesis 1:27,31. It is impossible for us to imagine a God who could exist, so to speak, *in vacuo*, without exercising his creative activity, and providing himself with objective demonstrations of his wisdom, power and love (Psalm 19:1. Isaiah 43:21. Matthew 6:28,29).

Cross

Death by crucifixion was practised by the Phoenicians and Carthaginians, and to a certain extent by the Romans, though in their case it was reserved only for slaves and the lowest types of criminal. No Roman citizen could suffer in this way—'Far be it

29

from a Roman citizen to behold a cross, let alone suffer on one'
(Cicero)—and it was finally abolished by the Emperor
Constantine. It was therefore a method of execution in use at the
time of Jesus's arrest and trial.

The Greek word *stauros* (cross) originally meant a stake, and
criminals were often nailed to a single stake fixed in the ground.
But the word is also used by ancient writers of the T-shaped cross
(Latin: *crux*), and from the earliest times Christian writers have
held that this was the cross on which Jesus was crucified.

Men decreed that Jesus should die in this particularly brutal and
humiliating manner (Philippians 2:8); but because of what his
death achieved for mankind, the cross has become the deeply
respected symbol of the Christian Faith, and the word is used
throughout the New Testament as a way of summarizing the 'full,
perfect and sufficient sacrifice, oblation and satisfaction for the
sins of the whole world' which Jesus Christ made on that first
Good Friday. The cross therefore has always been regarded by
Christians as the means of their salvation (Colossians 1:20; 2:14),
the central theme of their message for the world (1 Corinthians
1:17,18,23; 2:2), and the only thing in which they have any grounds
for boasting (Galatians 6:14).

The cross also touches the Christian's life at two other points. First,
he must 'be on it' (Galatians 2:20). This means that because Christ
died for our sins, they no longer have any rightful claim or
dominion over us. As far as they are concerned, we must no longer
seem to exist, and reckon ourselves 'to be dead to sin' (Romans
6:11).

Secondly, the Christian is told to 'take it up' (Matthew 16:24). This
is a way of saying that he must be willing to be identified with
Christ, and in some measure to share his shame and suffering, and
to stand up for him by bearing his reproach (Hebrews 13:13).

Curse

1. Sometimes the word had the force of an oath or a pledge, and
implied a wish to be punished by God or man if it were broken
(Nehemiah 10:29, AV, RSV. Acts 23:12 AV). As such it had much
the same force as when a person says 'Strike me dead if I don't . . .'

2. But far more commonly the word was used as the almost exact
opposite of a blessing—a malediction rather than a benediction: a
pronouncement of evil towards someone whom you disliked or
who had offended you (Job 31:30).

3. When the curse was uttered by God himself, it was a way of expressing his extreme displeasure, and was often accompanied by some visitation to show his disfavour towards the person or object concerned. We see examples of this in Zechariah 5:1-4, where God's curse is pictured as 'a flying scroll' (NEB) sweeping through the land, and again in the withering power of Christ's own pronouncement against the unfruitful fig tree (Mark 11:14,20,21).
4. There is finally a sense in which the word became personalised. The man or woman cursed were so identified with the malediction, that they themselves were spoken of as 'a curse' (Jeremiah 29:18. AV, RSV). We see this most strikingly expressed in Galatians 3:13,14 where we are told that Christ was 'made a curse for us', because in our place he accepted the outpouring of God's wrath against sin and demonstrated this by dying the type of death on which Deuteronomy 21:22,23 had pronounced a special curse. (See also 2 Corinthians 5:21.) It was of course only by allowing himself to suffer God's curse that Jesus made it possible for us to enjoy God's blessing which we had forfeited through sin.

D

Damnation
(See JUDGEMENT)

Darkness
Sometimes the word is used to describe the darkened path which the Christian must tread, and which is illuminated for him by the presence of Christ (John 8:12; 12:35. Psalms 18:28; 112:4); but more often it is employed as a synonym of some aspect of sin, particularly in the Gospel and first epistle of John (John 1:5. 1 John 1:5-7).
1. It is applied to the state of mind of those who are without God. We are told that 'their senseless minds were darkened' (Romans 1:21) and that 'they are darkened in their understanding' (Ephesians 4:18). Satan has blinded them with ignorance (2 Corinthians 4:4).
2. It also describes the behaviour and manner of life of such people. They 'walk in the ways of darkness' (Proverbs 2:13), for 'the way of the wicked is like deep darkness' (Proverbs 4:19); and they practise what Paul calls 'the unfruitful works of darkness' (Ephesians 5:11).
3. Finally, it describes their condition. They are pictured as prisoners of 'the power of darkness' (Colossians 1:13. Ephesians

6:12). It was to deliver mankind from this miserable condition that Christ came into the world (Isaiah 9:2) 'to open their eyes, and to turn them from darkness to light, and from the power of Satan unto God' (Acts 26:18 AV. 1 Peter 2:9).

Deacon
This is the name which came to be applied to the administrative officers of the Church. It is a translation of the Greek word *diakonos* which comes from a verb meaning to 'serve' or 'minister' (Mark 10:45). Very rarely therefore is it translated 'deacon' (Philippians 1:1. 1 Timothy 3:8,12), but nearly always 'servant' or 'minister' (Ephesians 3:7). It was often used by classical writers of a waiter at table.

In the New Testament there must have been some distinction between bishops and deacons, or they would not have been referred to separately by Paul, and it is interesting to note that women were allowed to become deaconesses but there is no reference to a woman as a bishop (Romans 16:1 RSV). As deaconesses there is nothing to connect them with the social responsibilities in Acts 6, and no hint from the description of their duties in 1 Timothy 3:8-13 of the particular functions they were later to assume.

Death
1. *Physical death.* Although fossil remains show that animals died millions of years ago, it would seem from the Genesis story that man would not have died if he had not sinned (Genesis 2.17). From the moment that he sinned, his body came under the same death-process as was in the rest of the animal world.

2. *Spiritual death.* This is the condition in which people exist who have never come into living personal contact with God through Jesus Christ; for 'he who has the Son has life; and he who has not the Son has not life' (1 John 5:12), but is 'dead in trespasses and sins' (Ephesians 2:1). Life in this new spiritual sense like physical life, comes through birth to those who have been 'born again' (John 3:3) through faith in Jesus Christ (John 1:11,12).

3. *Eternal death.* In this case death is not seen so much as a present state (though there is a sense in which it is that—John 3:18. Romans 6:23) as a future event, the final divine penalty for sin. The Bible does not describe it in terms of total extinction or annihilation, but says that 'those who refuse to acknowledge God and ... who will not obey the gospel of our Lord Jesus ... will suffer

the punishment of eternal ruin, cut off from the presence of the Lord and the splendour of his might' (2 Thessalonians 1:8,9 NEB). In other places too this final condition of unbelieving man is spoken of with great solemnity (Matthew 25:41 &c), and always in terms of suffering and separation.

It is important to note that Christ provided the answer to all three kinds of death; for he came to 'destroy him who has the power of death, that is, the devil' (Hebrews 2:14). First, he has 'brought life and immortality to light' (2 Timothy 1:10), and by rising again has shown that we need no longer fear physical death (1 Thessalonians 4:13,14). Secondly, through faith in Christ, the Christian begins to 'live' in a sense he never did before, in a new, spiritual dimension (John 10:10; 17:3). Thirdly, he can look forward eventually to being 'with Christ' (Philippians 1:23) and sharing in his everlasting immortality.

Debt
(See SIN)

Deliverance
(See SALVATION)

Demons
(See also SATAN)

Although the AV speaks of casting out 'devils', the Greek word is always *demons*. It seems clear from many places in the gospels that one of Satan's most vigorous ways of opposing the person and work of Christ was by using his 'agents' to 'possess' people; and that one of the ways in which Jesus most unmistakably demonstrated his divine power was by casting these demons out (Luke 11:20), and setting 'at liberty those who are oppressed' (Luke 4:18).

These agents or demons (which may have been separate beings or manifestations of the devil himself) as they are usually called did not produce normal forms of physical sickness, which are described quite separately in the narratives (Mark 1:34; 7:31-37. Luke 9:1), but caused things like aphasia or dumbness (Luke 11:14), epilepsy (Mark 9:17-29) and even a form of insanity (Luke 8:26-36).

The power Jesus showed in casting out these demons was also

delegated to his disciples (Luke 9:1), although he warned them not to get too excited about the success they met with in exercising it (Luke 10:17-20).

Disciple

The word means 'pupil' or 'student', and was applied to those who attached themselves to some well known teacher like John the Baptist (Matthew 9:14), Moses (John 9:28) and Gamaliel (Acts 22:3 NEB). It was natural therefore that it should have been used to describe the followers of Jesus, being applied first to the Twelve (Mark 3:14), and later to those who came to believe on Christ through their ministry (Matthew 28:19 RSV, NEB. Acts 11:26).

Doctrine

The noun 'doctrine' comes from the verb 'to teach'. In other words, 'doctrine' is 'what is taught'. Gradually this teaching became crystallised into a body of doctrine or 'pattern of teaching' (Romans 6:17 NEB), and even into a kind of 'mini-creed' (1 Corinthians 15:3,4); and one test of true discipleship was steadfast continuance in this doctrine (Titus 1:9. 2 John 9), despite the prevalence of 'all sorts of outlandish teachings' (Hebrews 13:9 NEB).

As time went on, a certain amount of specialisation became inevitable, and we find that some men were particularly gifted as teachers (1 Corinthians 12:28,29. Ephesians 4:11). They were able to impart doctrine clearly and simply, and to train others to do the same (2 Timothy 2:2).

Doubt

(See UNBELIEF)

E

Earnest
(See GUARANTEE)

Elder
This word finds its parallel in many communities, and refers to the senior members in whom was invested a certain amount of authority. In Old Testament days the word was frequently used to describe leaders among the Children of Israel (Deuteronomy 29:10; 31:28 &c), and it was they who, in later years, under the Ruler of the Synagogue (Luke 13:14), probably guided local church affairs.

It was natural therefore that the word should have been taken over into the New Testament and applied to those who held positions of leadership within the Christian Church. Preaching, teaching (1 Timothy 5:17) and healing (James 5:14) seem to have been among their principal functions, but there was no very marked specialisation at this stage, nothing to indicate the office of 'presbyter' or 'priest' into which they were to develop, and nothing to distinguish them from bishops (see article).

Election
Our own popular use of the word today tends to obscure its meaning in the Bible, where it indicated originally the free,

36

personal and sovereign choice by God of the Children of Israel. In fact both RSV and NEB prefer the word 'chosen' to 'elected', and Israel is spoken of as 'my chosen' (Isaiah 42:1).

This choice is attributed in the Old Testament (a) to God's unexpected and unmerited love (Deuteronomy 7:7; 23:5) and (b) to his desire to use his chosen people to bring him glory by witnessing to him before the other nations of the world (Psalm 102:16-18. Isaiah 43:21; 55:5). It was because this purpose could only be fulfilled by a righteous nation, that God had to discipline his people, and at times deal so severely with them.

In the New Testament it is the Christian Church, largely composed of non-Jews, which inherits the privileges of election, and Paul explains that its members are grafted into the main trunk of the tree in place of some of the natural branches which, because of their unbelief and disobedience, have been broken off (Romans 11:16-24). The New Testament makes no attempt to dilute or to explain the fact of God's sovereign and personal choice of some people to share in the experience of everlasting life (Romans 8:29. Ephesians 1:5,9), while others are destined to be excluded (Romans 9:18-22), any more than Old Testament writers can account for his preference for Israel. We know from other passages of the Bible that this pre-destination is perfectly compatible with freedom of choice on the part of individual people (Matthew 11:28-30. Revelation 22:17), and the Christian humbly accepts the paradox, confident that 'the judge of all the earth' will 'do what is just' (Genesis 18:25 NEB).

To the Christian believer this doctrine can bring comfort and confidence. It reminds him that his salvation does not depend upon his own choice so much as upon God's choice of him (John 15:16); that his eternal security is fully guaranteed (Romans 8:35-39); and because of this confidence, he is inspired to live for God in a positive and purposeful way (Colossians 3:12-17).

There is also a special sense in which God chooses individual people for a particular task. Moses (Psalm 106:23), Jeremiah (Jeremiah 1:5) and Paul (Acts 9:15) are good examples of the way in which, throughout history, God has matched his moments with his men.

Epistle

Originally the word meant a written communication between two people—what we would call a letter, and this word is preferred in

37

modern translations. But the personal details the New Testament letters contain (with certain exceptions) are few, and probably their nearest counterpart today would be a Bishop's Diocesan Letter, or perhaps a letter to the local press.

In one place Paul uses the word metaphorically when, to those who expected him to produce letters of introduction, he claims that his Christian converts were living epistles, available for all to reed (2 Corinthians 3:1-3).

Eternity

The noun occurs only once in the Bible, and then only in the AV and RSV (Isaiah 57:15), but the adjective 'eternal' or 'everlasting' is frequently applied to God (see article) and his attributes (Deuteronomy 33:27. Jeremiah 31:3). The simplest meaning of the word is 'timelessness'. To emphasise this it sometimes appears in the plural form (Psalm 145:13), and in the New Testament the phrase 'to the ages of the ages', or 'for ever and ever' (Galatians 1:5 &c) is intended to express the idea of an endless unfolding series of immeasurable periods.

The Hebrew word for eternity also began to acquire an idea connected with space as well as time, and this may account for the AV rendering of Mark 10:30 as 'the *world* to come' rather than 'the *age* to come'. In other words, God 'inhabits eternity' (Isaiah 57:15), living outside our space-time framework rather as an author is outside the book or play he has written. He may produce and direct it, and even for a time take a part; but essentially he belongs to a world which is dimensionally different, and in which ideas of space and time can find no sensible reference point.

Finally we must notice that it is in Jesus Christ that this new, eternal dimension of existence becomes available to man. The transition from ordinary human life to eternal life is not made at death, but at the moment when a man enters a personal relationship with Christ by faith (John 17:3).

Evil

This word is used more widely than 'sin', and includes everything that is naturally, physically and morally bad rather than good; though there is often a close relationship between these three aspects, and many disasters and much suffering are attributable to man's selfishness, greed and pride.

In so far as man himself is responsible, the problem of evil presents no great difficulty, because the only way in which the possibility could have been eliminated would have been the creation of a race of robots or automata, incapable of free will. In making man as he did, God must have foreseen the outcome, and the fact is that from his first act of disobedience (Genesis 3:6), man has been prone to choose evil rather than good.

It is much more difficult to explain the evil in the world which cannot be traced or attributed to man. However far back we push it, to rebellious and fallen angels and to 'the evil one' himself, we are in the end faced with the fact that God must have caused it. Indeed, the Hebrew mind made no difficulty out of this, and, discarding secondary causes, put the responsibility fairly and squarely upon God himself (Isaiah 45:7. Amos 3:6)

No explanation was offered, beyond the fact that God sometimes uses natural disasters to discipline his people (Amos 4:6-11; Haggai 1:6-11; 1 Peter 1:6,7) and to punish the disobedient (Matthew 9:2; Acts 5:5; 13:11). Though we must not suppose that all who suffer natural disasters are guilty of some special sin (Luke 13:4). See also the Book of Job.

Also we must not conclude from Isaiah 45:7 and Amos 3:6 that God is responsible for sin. 'Evil' (AV) in these verses means disaster which comes as discipline, as the context shows, and as the RSV and NEB indicate by translating as 'woe', 'trouble', 'disaster'.

It may perhaps be questioned whether some of the finest qualities of which man is capable—such things as courage and compassion—would be possible in a world in which there were no evil; and even whether the grace of God could have been expressed if there were no sin (Romans 5:19-21); but these are speculative questions and Christians have always preferred to see in the cross and in the revelation of a suffering God, personally identified with the evil in the world, a practical answer to the problem of evil which no philosopher has yet been able to find.

Expiation
(See PROPITIATION)

F

Faith

'And what is faith? Faith gives substance to our hopes, and makes us certain of realities we do not see' (Hebrews 11:1 NEB). In other words, we might compare ito the title-deeds of a house which we possess, but do not at present occupy.

Although the word 'faith' occurs vey rarely in the Old Testament, the idea is frequently present in such words as 'trust' or 'believe', while in the New Testament the word itself and the verb from which it is derived—'to believe'—appear on almost every page. There seem to be three main aspects of the word.

1. *Intellectual assent.* In this case it is facts which are believed rather than persons (Hebrews 11:3), and faith of this sort is not the exclusive experience of Christians, because we are told, concerning the existence of God, that 'even the demons believe, and shudder' (James 2:19).

2. *Personal committal.* Here the word is often followed by the preposition 'into' or 'upon', and suggests a continuing attitude of personal trust in Christ (John 3:16; 14:1 &c).

3. *Practical living.* Faith in Christ must reveal itself, and indeed can only be recognized for what it is, in a life which is pleasing to him. This is the great contribution which James makes to the

40

subject (James 2:15-26). Faith without deeds is a lifeless thing, a fact which the Old Testament writers themselves had already grasped (Psalm 37:3).

Faith is represented throughout the Bible as the 'master key' to all kinds of Christian experience. Indeed without it we cannot begin to please God (Hebrews 11:6). It opens the gate to personal salvation (John 3:16. Romans 5:1. Ephesians 2:5-8); to victory over temptation (1 Pe 5:8,9. 1 John 5:4); to answered prayer (Matthew 21:22. James 1:6); and to successful Christian progress (2 Corinthians 5:7. 1 Timothy 1:19).

Small wonder therefore that faith was the lesson that Jesus was most eager to teach, and his followers most anxious to learn, though sometimes all too slowly! 'Have you no faith?' (Mark 4:40), he asked. 'Have faith in God' (Mark 11:22) and 'when the Son of Man cometh shall he find faith on the earth?' (Luke 18:8 AV). 'Lord, increase our faith', they replied (Luke 17:5), and 'Lord, I believe, help my unbelief' (Mark 9:24). But faith does not arrive and grow automatically. 'Faith comes by hearing, and heering by the word of God' (Romans 10:17); 'by the preaching of Christ' (RSV). In other words, the more we learn about God through his word, the stronger our faith will become. The more we know of the one we have come to trust, the more trustworthy we find him to be.

Finally, there are two specialised senses in which the word is used. 'The gift of faith' (1 Corinthians 12:4-9) does seem to imply some sort of special endowment, perhaps for a particular purpose or task. 'The faith' (Jude 3) suggests that whathas been handed down and believed by Christians has coalesced into an accepted body of doctrine (see article), and become their Creed or Faith. It is in this sense that we often speak today about 'The Christian Faith'.

Fall

Nowhere does the Bible depict man to be rising steadily from a condition of moral squalor towards perfection, but exactly the reverse. Because of his disobedience (Genesis 3), he has forfeited the three things which he was created by God to enjoy: spiritual fellowship with God himself, moral excellence and material prosperity, including personal ascendancy over the natural creation.

The poison of sin has infected the whole human race (Romans 5:12. 1 Corinthians 15:21,22) so that 'there is none righteous, no, not one', 'for all have sinned, and fall short of the glory of God'

41

(Romans 3:12, 23). Everyone born into the world (Psalm 51:5) since the days of man's first disobedience has inherited this fatal flaw in his make-up, this natural tendency towards sin, which only Christ can counteract.

But the image of God in which man was originally created (Genesis 1:27), though badly damaged and tarnished, has not been wholly extinguished (1 Corinthians 11:7. James 3:9) and is not completely unrecognizable. Conscience (see article) is still at work (Romans 2:14,15. 2 Corinthians 4:2), reasonoay etill be apleaed to (Isaiah 1:18), and man still possesses the capacity of free will and is able to choose (Deuteronomy 30:19).

When Jesus Christ as 'a second Adam to the fight and to the rescue came', he did so in order to undo through his death and resurrection the effect of the fall. For the believer in him, therefore, 'a new creation' takes place (2 Corinthians 5:17), friendship with God is restored (1 Peter 3:18), and once again he may begin to 'walk in newness of life' (Romans 6:4.

Father
(See GOD and ABBA)

Favour
(See GRACE)

Fear
'The fear of the Lord' is a phrase which seems to stretch from something like terror at one extreme (Genesis 35:5. 2 Corinthians 5:11 AV) to loving trust at the other (Psalm 34:7-10). It includes the dread which the unrepentant should feel at the threat of judgement and the reverent and awesome respect of the Christian for a great and majestic God who is his heavenly Father.

We might compare it to the feelings we experience when confronted with some of the elemental forces of nature, such as fire, wind and sea. They vary from love at one extreme to dread at the other, and we can find no suitable word to cover the whole spectrum.

But 'the fear of the Lord' is more than just an emotional reaction. It closely affects our daily living. It comprises 'the whole duty of man' (Ecclesiastes 12:13). It is the one sure secret of wisdom (Psalm 111:10), and it carries with it a hatred of all that is evil (Proverbs 8:13).

Fellowship

This word, which is sometimes translated 'communion', 'participation' or 'sharing' (compare1 Corinthians 10:16 AV and NEB) is used in two senses in the New Testament. First, it refers to the union which exists between Christ and the Christian (1 John 1:3,7): a union which is in one place compared to marriage (Ephesians 5:25-27); and secondly it describes the union which Christians enjoy with each other (Acts 2:42 AV). But Christian fellowship is not only receptive, for it involves an active participation or sharing in objective experiences. Thus it is found and enjoyed in the sharing of the Lord's Supper (1 Corinthians 10:16), in the work of the Holy Spirit (Philippians 2:1), in active Christian service (2 Corinthians 8:4. Philippians 1:5) and in suffering for the sake of Christ (Philippians 3:10). In all these ways Christians may be drawn into a deeper and closer personal relationship with each other as well as with the Lord.

Flesh

The Bible uses this word in at least two distinct ways, one natural and the other technical.

1. *Natural.* In this sense it refers to normal human or animal existence. We read for example that Jesus 'became flesh' (John 1:14), meaning that he assumed our humanity; and that 'all flesh is grass' (Isaiah 40:6), which suggests the temporary, transient nature of human life.

2. *Technical.* In the New Testament Paul uses the word to describe that ineradicable bias towards sin which is in every man. The NEB calls it the 'unspiritual' part of us or our 'lower nature' in which there is no goodness (Romans 7:18) or power to please God (Romans 8:8. Matthew 26:41). The flesh must not be identified with the body (which is good, and must be cared for—Ephesians 5:29), nor with our temperament or human nature as such, which God intends us to use positively in his service. The flesh is the moral poison which has entered our personalities, polluting at every level. To change the metaphor, the flesh is the usurper who has gained control of the country which does not belong to him by right, and now stands in direct opposition to the Spirit, that new occupying force who has come to live within the heart of the Christian.

The Christian himself has therefore become a battleground in which the flesh and the Spirit strive for the mastery of his will

(Romans 7:18-25. Galatians 5:17), and it is only by allying himself continually with tte latter that he can enjoy victory (Romans 8:2). In practice this meens a conscious and deliberate determination with God's help to 'abstain from the passions of the flesh' (1 Peter 2:11 RSV), to 'make no provision for the flesh to gratify its desires' (Romans 13:14 RSV); but rather to 'walk in the Spirit' (Galatians 5:16 AV) and to be 'led by the Spirit' (Romans 8:14 AV).

Forgiveness

In the Old Testament we learn that God's forgiveness springs from his love, but if man is to enjoy it he must be willing to repent and forsake his evil ways (Exodus 34:6,7. Isaiah 55:7). We see its measure and scope in some of the metaphors used, for we are told that our sins have been put out of sight (Isaiah 38:17. Micah 7:19), out of reach (Psalm 103:12), out of mind (Jeremiah 31:34) and out of account (Psalm 103:10).

In the New Testament easily the most frequently used word for forgiveness is *aphiemi* which means to send away, dismiss or release, and carries with it most of the ideas contained in the Old Testament metaphors. It is the removal of a burden and a stain which brings relief to the sinner, and makes possible the renewal of friendship. Perhaps the most perfect picture in the New Testament is found in the story of the Prodigal Son (Luke 15), where the young man was not only received back, but restored.

But forgiveness is costly, and there are many reminders in the New Testament that it has only been made possible for us through the death of Christ upon the cross (Matthew 26:28. Ephesians 1:7), and that 'he died that we might be forgiven'.

God's forgiveness of us (which has no limits—Matthew 18:21-35) is closely linked with our readiness to forgive those who offend us (Matthew 18:23-35); for the person who withholds his forgiveness from another has not properly repented and to that extent does not qualify for God's forgiveness of himself (Luke 6:37. Colossians 3:13).

Fruit

Apart from its literal use, and when the word is sometimes found as a synonym for children (Psalm 127:3 AV, RSV. Luke 1:42), 'fruit' is a familiar Bible metaphor for spiritual progress, particularly in the realm of personal moral conduct.

Perhaps the best known passage is Galatians 5:22,23 where 'the fruit of the Spirit' is described; while elsewhere we read of 'fruit that befits repentance' (Matthew 3: 8), 'fruit unto holiness' (Romans 6:22 AV), 'the fruit of light' (Ephesians 5:9) and the 'fruits of righteousness' (Philippians 1:11). Such fruit is not generated from the natural man, but grows from our close personal relationship with Christ, which John describes as 'abiding' or 'dwelling' in him (John 15:1-16).

Very occasionally the word seems to be used f the harvest which the Christian worker reaps as he preaches the gospel (Romans 1:13), and Paul on one occasion speaks of 'fruitful labour' (Philippians 1:22). The metaphor may have been suggested by Jesus' reference to the world as a harvest field awaiting the arrival of more labourers (Matthew 9:35-38).

Glory

The glory of something is its intrinsic worth, value or splendour. The glory of a sunset is its beauty, of a craftsman his skill and of a lion its strength; and the glory of God lies in his character of holiness and love, wisdom and power.

In the Old Testament people were given passing glimpses of this eternal glory. They saw it in the miracles he performed in Egypt (Numbers 14:21,22), in the cloud that led them through the wilderness (Exodus 16:7,10), and they sensed it in his coming to the tabernacle (Exodus 40:34-38). Later Jews spoke of this visible glory as the 'Shekinah' with a root meaning of 'to rest', as the cloud rested on the tabernacle. And they also, like everyone else, including ourselves, were aware of God's glory in the created universe (Psalm 19:1-6).

Turning to the New Testament, we find that the glory of God is almost exclusively associated with the person and work of the Lord Jesus Christ, and we are told that 'God was glorified in him' (John 13:31). He was described as 'reflecting the glory of God' (Hebrews 1:3), and while no one has ever seen God, we are given 'the light of the knowledge of the glory of God in the face of Jesus Christ' (2 Corinthians 4:6).

Supremely, perhaps, this glory was demonstrated at his

46

transfiguration (Luke 9:28-3y), when Peter, James and John were 'eye-witnesses of his majesty' (2 Peter 1:16-18), at his death (John 12:23,24), resurrection (Romans 6:4) and ascension (Acts 7:55). It was no doubt of these occasions particularly that John was thinking when many years later he wrote, 'And we beheld his glory, the glory as of the only begotten of the Father, full of grace and truth' (John 1:14).

It is important to remember that man too was made 'in the image and glory of God' (1 Corinthians 11:7), though through his sin, he has been 'deprived of the divine splendour' (Romans 3:23 NEB). But one of the great purposes of our redemption is that we should again be 'shaped to the likeness of his Son' (Romans 8:29 NEB), and begin to 'reflect as in a mirror the splendour of the Lord' (2 Corinthians 3:18 NEB).

God

In its grandly simple opening verse, the Bible makes no attempt to explain the existence of God (Genesis 1:1), but assumes that he is the self-conscious, self-sufficient, uncaused cause of all things; the Bible assumes also that he is able to reveal himself and communicate with his creatures.

These two facts about God are seen in the two Hebrew words used in the Old Testament to describe him. *El* contains the basic idea of God, and usually appears with an adjective such as *El elyon*, or 'most high God', while *Jahveh* (or Yahweh) or 'Jehovah' (often translated 'LORD' in capital letters) gives us the more personal idea of his character, and is particularly associated with his redemption of his people at the Red Sea. Sometimes we find them both together, as for example in Genesis 2:5-9, where we read that 'The LORD God formed man . . .'

Beginning therefore with the early chapters of Genesis, it is not long before we start to see what God is like, although the picture is not complete until we reach the New Testament.

1. *God is Spirit* (John 4:24). This means that he is without a body or a physical presence of any sort, and therefore indiscernible to human sight or hearing (1 Timothy 1:17. John 1:18) in his absolute Being, although he may assume a form in which he can be seen (Isaiah 6:1). He transcends the universe he has created, and yet he pervades it (Acts 17:28). He is completely independent of space and time (Isaiah 57:15), a fact that was revealed for Moses by the name by which he called himself—the eternal 'I AM' (Exodus 3:14), and

47

yet he can invade and use both at any moment he chooses. Like the wind (the Greek word for 'wind' is the same as 'spirit') he is everywhere present, as the psalmist discovered (Psalm 139:7-12); but can be enjoyed by the individual as if he had all of him there was (Joshua 1:5,9).

2. *God is light* (1 John 1:5) 'and in him is no darkness at all.' Light and darkness (see article) are Bible metaphors for good and evil, and from this we learn that God is utterly holy (Exodus 15:11. Leviticus 11:44; 19:2). In one place we read that 'the Lord God has sworn by his holiness' (Amos 4:2), as though that was his greatest and most impressive attribute. Isaiah, at the beginning of his prophetic ministry, was given a glimpse of this unutterable holiness, and was overwhelmed with a sense of unworthiness and shame (Isaiah 6:1-8). Nothing that is remotely tainted with evil can stand in his presence or survive when his righteous anger is kindled; 'for the LORD your God is a consuming fire' (Deuteronomy 4:24), and 'can any of us live with a devouring fire?' (Isaiah 33:14 NEB).

3. *God is love* (1 John 4:8). This love is seen in his creative activity, in the way he sustains life (Acts 17:28), sending his rain on good and bad alike (Matthew 5:45), and giving 'us richly all things to enjoy' (1 Timothy 6:17). It is seen again in his gracious choice of Israel (Deuteronomy 7:7) and in the fatherly way in which he watched over her interests. We see this love supremely, not only in our 'creation, preservation and all the blessings of this life,' but in the way in which God gave his Son to be the Saviour of the world; for 'in this was manifested the love of God toward us, because that God sent his only begotten Son into the world, that we might live through him' (1 John 4:9 AV). And finally, we see his love in the way he has adopted us into his family, and allowed us to address him as 'Father' (1 John 3:2. Romans 8:15).

It is very difficult for the human mind to think intelligibly about a God who on the one hand is so isolated from us and on the other so involved with us; and there were times in the Old Testament when first one aspect was emphasised and then another, and human words could hardly take the strain. We are told in one place that 'Heaven itself, the highest heaven cannot contain thee' (1 Kings 8:27 NEB); in other places he is spoken of almost as we might speak of another man, and credited with human moods, feelings and apparent changeability (Genesis 6:6); but these are figures of speech, and an accommodation to our human viewpoint.

48

It is in the person of Jesus Christ that the two are seen to coalesce—the eternal and the personal. Those who came to know him, realized that he belonged to a world they had never known (Luke 9:28-36), and differed from them not just in degree, but also in kind; and yet at the same time he was someone whom they could meet and know as a living personal friend (1 John 1·1,2), with temptations, feelings and interests just like their own.

Nature can teach us much about the wisdom, power and goodness of God (Psalm 19:1-6. Romans 1:20), but it is only in the person of Jesus Christ himself that we see what he is really like; and looking at him, men realized that what they saw was someone in whom 'the complete being of the Godhead dwells embodied' (Colossians 2:9 NEB). Jesus was the living prism through whom the invisible light of the world (Colossians 1:15) was presented to mankind in terms which they could appreciate and understand with their limited and imperfect human faculties (John 1:18; 14:9. 2 Corinthians 4:6).

Godliness
(See also RELIGION)
'Manliness' is the word we apply to someone who exhibits manly qualities, and in the same way 'Godliness' describes someone whose life is godly. It is a favourite word of Paul's, and occurs often in his pastoral epistles (1 Timothy 2:2; 3:16; 4:7,8; 6:3,5,6,11 &c). Some modern translations (including the NEB) use the word 'religion' (see article) instead of godliness, perhaps because the Greek word (*eusebia*) includes the idea of order and discipline as well as holiness of life, and this is felt to make the former word more appropriate.

Good(ness)
The word is applied throughout the Bible to everything that gives moral, spiritual or physical satisfaction. Thus it was a 'good land' (Deuteronomy 8:7) which God had prepared for his people, 'good wine' which was produced at the wedding at Cana (John 2:10), a 'good work' or 'beautiful act' which Mary performed for Jesus (Matthew 26:10), and Barnabas was described as 'a good man' (Acts 11:24). In each case the adjective expresses pleasure in and approval of the noun.

1. *Applied to God.* When the Biblical writers refer to God as good, it is not that they assess him according to any preconceived idea of goodness they may have, 'but rather that contemplating the supreme glory of God's perfections, they apply to him the ordinary

49

word for acknowledging worth. By doing so, however, they give that word a new depth of meaning. They define good in terms of God: not vice versa' (Dr. J. I. Packer).

From this'simple statement that 'the Lord is good' (Nahum 1:7), it follows logically that what God does is good also—'Thou art good and (thou) doest good' (Psalm 119:68). His creation is good (Genesis 1:31), his gifts to mankind are good (Matthew 7:11. James 1:17). His ordinances are good (Psalm 119:39), and so are his commandments (Romans 7:12), his will (Romans 12:2), his purposes (Romans 8:28) and his promises (1 Kings 8:56).

2. *Applied to man.* The word 'good' cannot be applied to man in his natural condition, because every part of him—thought, feelings and will—is tainted with the poison of sin. 'There is none that doeth good, no, not one' (Romans 3:12; 7:18). That is why Jesus replied as he did to the young man who addressed him as '*Good* Master' (Matthew 19:16,17); he was saying, in effect, 'If you are calling me good, then you are equating me with God.' But goodness is one of the fruits of the Spirit (Galatians 5:22), and if the Spirit is living in the heart of the Christian believer, he will begin to produce it, so that it should become true of him that he is 'full of goodness' (Romans 15:14). The result will be that what he does will be good, and in the New Testament we find great emphasis on the 'good works' expected of the Christian (Matthew 5:14-16. Ephesians 2:10. Colossians 1:10. Titus 2:14). He will find too that he begins to enjoy a good conscience (1 Timothy 1:5), and in the course of time will acquire a good name (Proverbs 22:1).

Gospel

This is the word used to translate the Greek word *euangelion*, meaning 'good story' or 'good news'. (It was used, for example, with reference to the birthday of the Emperor Augustus). The Anglo-Saxon word 'god' meant 'God' if the 'o' was short and 'good' if it was long. In this way the 'Good story' became the 'God story', 'God-spell' or 'Gospel'.

1. *The gospel foretold.* The good news did not burst upon a world which was totally unprepared for it, because watchful, Godfearing people realized that it came as the fulfilment of many Old Testament prophecies (Romans 1:1,2. Isaiah 7:14; 53; 61:1-3). Both Zacharias and Simeon came to understand that they were witnessing the beginning of God's great act of redemption (Luke 1:67-79; 2:26-32); and to the shepherds also, as a representative

50

group of ordinary people, there were announced in advance the 'good tidings of great joy' (Luke 2:9-11 AV).

2. *The gospel explained.* What began in the teaching of Jesus as 'the gospel of the kingdom' (Matthew 4:23) became 'the gospel of your salvation' (Ephesians 1:13), because it was only through his death upon the cross that Jesus could bring deliverance from the guilt and power of sin, and open the Kingdom of heaven to all believers; the subject of the gospel message became the King himself rather than the Kingdom. The gospel was at one and the same time a demonstration of God's grace (Acts 20:24) and his power (Romans 1:16). The grace was seen in the love which took Jesus to the cross; and the power in his conquest of Satan, sin and death.

3. *The gospel proclaimed.* Among Jesus' last commands was one to 'preach the gospel' (Mark 16:15 AV, RSV. Matthew 28:19) and his followers ever since have regarded it as their privilege and their responsibility to help a lost world to find the Saviour (2 Corinthians 4:4). Paul felt a tremendous compulsion to do this (1 Corinthians 9:16), regarding the gospel as a sacred trust (1 Timothy 1:11) of which he must never be ashamed (Romans 1:16. Ephesians 6:19), and for the sake of which he must be ready to accept hardship and suffering (1 Thessalonians 2:2. 2 Timothy 1:8).

Grace

The word comes from a verb suggesting free, unrivalled action, and means 'Favour'. It can only be used of God's attitude to man, and never vice versa, because we cannot in any circumstances 'do God a favour'. To 'Say Grace' at meals, for example, is to acknowledge a favour from God by giving him thanks. The Old Testament is full of the idea of God's grace, expressed either by the word itself (Jeremiah 31:2), or by a closely related word (Lamentations 3:22); while in the Gospels many of the stories illustrate the meaning of the word (e.g. Luke 15:11-24), even though it is not actually used by Jesus himself.

It is in the epistles that it gains most prominence, where we are told that 'the grace of God that bringeth salvation hath appeared to all men' (Titus 2:11 AV); and we learn that it is through God's grace, his undeserved favour, that we are saved from sin (Ephesians 2:8-10) and justified in his sight (Romans 3:24). Grace is always

51

contrasted with Law (Romans 6:14), for it is by God's favour and not our own merit that we are justified.

But the operation of God's favour towards us does not stop with our salvation, and although this is the primary use of the word, and Paul speaks of 'the gospel of the grace of God' (Acts 20:24), it is applied to other situations as well. For example, God 'favoured' Paul with the strength to live under some sort of physical handicap (2 Corinthians 12:9,10); with the privilege of preaching the gospel to the Gentiles (Ephesians 3:8); and with the particular gifts which he needed for his ministry (Ephesians 4:7). Peter in his turn reminds us that grace can only be given to the humble (1 Peter 5:5), to those who are willing to accept a favour; and that we are to grow in our experience of God's grace towards us (2 Peter 3:18). No wonder the word should have found its place in the most frequently used of all benedictions (2 Corinthians 13:14)!

Guarantee

This word is only found in three places in the New Testament, and while the RSV translates it 'guarantee', the NEB has 'pledge' and the AV 'earnest'. It is a commercial word of Semitic origin and was the deposit ('earnest money') paid when something was purchased, as a guarantee that the rest of what was promised would follow. We might compare it to the practice of Hire Purchase in this country today. In its feminine form it later came to mean an engagement ring, the pledge of future marriage.

In the New Testament it is applied to the Holy Spirit, for his presence in the heart of the Christian believer is the guarantee and the first instalment of the full salvation which will become his when at last he goes to be with Christ (2 Corinthians 1:22; 5:5. Ephesians 1:14).

Guilt
(See SIN)

Heart

This word is nearly always used in the Bible in a metaphorical sense, to suggest the centre of the personality, just as today we might speak of getting to 'the heart' of a matter, or refer to people as 'half-hearted' or 'warm-hearted'.

It is a kind of 'parliament' of a person's life, where thoughts arise (Luke 24:38), where feelings are experienced (Luke 24:32) of anxiety (John 14:1), sorrow (John 16:6) and joy (Isaiah 65:14). It is that part of us which is capable of belief (Romans 10:9) and unbelief (Hebrews 3:12), and where the will makes its decisions (2 Corinthians 9:7). It follows from this that the state of a man's heart affects his whole life, for 'as he thinks in his heart so is he' (Proverbs 23:7), and 'from it flow the springs of life' (Proverbs 4:23).

It is natural therefore that man's disobedience and sinfulness should be traced back to the heart, for it is there, from the heart, that there proceed the sins listed in Matthew 15:18,19; and it is small wonder that Jeremiah should describe the human heart as 'desperately sick' (Jeremiah 17:9).

If man is to be redeemed and restored, therefore, his heart must be put right and renewed (Ezekiel 18:31; 36:26). It must be enlightened (2 Corinthians 4:6), cleansed (Hebrews 10:22. Psalm 51:10) and filled with love for God (Romans 5:5). Only then will it seek after him and want to know him (Jeremiah 24:7) and to do his will (Romans 6:17).

Heaven
(See also RESURRECTION)
In some places in the Bible the word 'Heaven' (or 'Heavens') is used to distinguish the rest of the universe from the small corner of it on which we live, namely earth (Genesis 1:1. Psalm 19:1. Matthew 5:18); but much more often it is the name given to the dwelling-place of God himself (Deuteronomy 26:15. Matthew 5:45) where he is attended by his holy angels, that 'multitude of the heavenly host' (Mark 13:32. Luke 2:13). This is the place to which Jesus returned after his ascension (Acts 1:11), and it is as living there that we must think of him today (Acts 7:56 AV), representing us in the presence of his Father (Hebrews 9:24) and preparing the place which God has appointed for all those who love him (John 14:2,3. 1 Peter 1:4).
It is in the Book of Revelation that we read most about Heaven, and though the language is highly figurative and symbolic, there is much that we can learn. We find, for example, that in the new heaven and new earth there will be *no sea* (Revelation 21:1), because the sea stands for separation and destruction, and Heaven is a place where God's people are for ever united, and where 'partings are no more'. There will be *no sun* (Revelation 21:23), because we shall be in the presence of the Creator of the sun, and 'the glory of God is its light'. Finally, there will be *no sin* (Revelation 21:27), and we are told that nothing which is unclean shall enter it (see Psalm 24:3-5). It is these facts, symbolically expressed for us, which are more important to understand and appreciate than the precise whereabouts of Heaven, or its nature and dimensions; and as is so often the case, the Bible gives us the essential truths—enough to live on because it knows that finite human minds cannot fully grasp infinite and eternal concepts.

Hell
To try to understand this subject properly, we must introduce ourselves to four words:
1. *Sheol.* This is the word used in the Old Testament to describe the place to which people go when they die (Psalm 88:3. Isaiah 38:18). It means 'the place of shades' and was therefore looked upon with horror as a place to shun (Psalm 16:10), because physical death in itself was regarded as the penalty for sin.

2. *Hades.* This is the equivalent word in the New Testament, and is sometimes translated simply as 'death' (Matthew 16:18 RSV, NEB), but in Acts 2:27, 31 (RSV) it is rendered 'Hades'. It is this word which is paraphrased as 'Hell' in the Apostles' Creed, thus giving rise to some confusion of thought.

3. *Paradise.* The word means 'garden'. It is used only in a literal sense in the Old Testament, but in the New Testament it appears three times metaphorically, and is probably simply a descriptive word of the place to which God's people go immediately after departing this life. The most famous instance is Luke 23:43, where Jesus promises the dying thief that he will join him 'in paradise' that same day.

4. *Gehenna.* The word is derived from 'The Valley of Hinnom', the name given to the refuse dump outside the city which had once been a centre of idolatry (Jeremiah 7:31). It was used in the New Testament to describe the place where the wicked must suffer the penalty of eternal death (Matthew 10:28. Romans 6:23), or what Paul calls 'the punishment of eternal destruction and exclusion from the presence of the Lord' (2 Thessalonians 1:9 RSV). However much the mind may shrink from the thought of such a fate prepared for the wicked, the Bible refuses to dilute its teaching on this subject to accommodate human feelings.

Heresy

The word really means 'choice', and has come to stand for any deviation by a person or a party from the orthodox and accepted Faith of the Christian Church. The Greek word (*hairesis*) is translated in various ways in the English versions, such as 'sect', 'faction', 'dissension', as well as 'heresy'.

The Christians had of course been regarded by orthodox Jews as heretics, and were harassed and hounded as such (Acts 24:5,14; 28:22), but it was not long before they found themselves up against the same problem, and faced with what Peter called 'disastrous heresies' (2 Peter 2:1 NEB). At this stage these took three principal forms. First, there were those who tried to add to Christianity a great many doctrines and philosophical ideas which did not belong to it, and only confused and misled people (Colossians 2:8-23); secondly, those who attempted to take from it one of its most fundamental truths, namely, that when Jesus came to this earth he really did assume a truly human body (1 John 4:2,3. 2 John 7); and thirdly, those who tried to make the gospel an adjunct of the Law by insisting that Christians must submit to circumcision and other Jewish rites (Galatians 1:6-9; 2:11-21; 5:2-12).

Paul regarded such heresies as the direct outcome of sinful, unspiritual human nature—'the works of the flesh' (Galatians 5:19-21 AV, RSV). It led him to issue strong and careful instructions to those in positions of Christian leadership (Titus 3:10); and it led him also to stress the basic importance of Christian unity—a unity founded on the presence of the Holy Spirit within the heart of every Christian (Ephesians 4:3) and upon adherence to the same great Christian truths (Ephesians 4:13).

Holiness

The root idea of this word in both Old Testament and New Testament seems to be negatively of separation from all that is evil and positively of consecration to God. It was applied to things as well as to people (Exodus 3:5; 20:8; 30:35. Psalm 93:5), and signified the special purpose to which the day or place or article was to be dedicated.

The holiness of God (see article) receives very great emphasis in the Bible, and accounts for the elaborate ritual with which he was approached. It was because he was so unutterably holy (Leviticus 19:2. Isaiah 6:3), that man is required to be holy too (Leviticus 20:7. 1 Peter 1:15,16); for holiness is the one thing without which no one will be allowed into God's presence (Hebrews 12:14).

But personal holiness is not something that we can produce naturally; for we 'were by nature the children of wrath' (Ephesians 2:3). Therefore there has to be a 'new nature, created after the likeness of God in true righteousness and holiness' (Ephesians 4:24)—a sharing of his holiness (Hebrews 12:10); and the work which is begun in this way, is continued by the operation of the Holy Spirit in our hearts and lives (1 Corinthians 6:19,20).

Holy Spirit

In the Old Testament the Holy Spirit usually revealed himself as a kind of temporary power, bestowed for special purposes (Judges 14:6. 1 Samuel 10:10). At Pentecost, however, he came down permanently to work in a new way (John 7:39), and to abide for ever (John 14:16) in the Church as the life of the body (1 Corinthians 12) and in the individual Christian as the source of his new spiritual life (1 Corinthians 6:19).

From the New Testament we find that;

1. *He is personal.* He is always spoken of as as a Person (Romans 8:26

AV is a mis-translation) and not a thing or an influence. Jesus referred to him in this way (John 16:13), because he is as much one person of the triune God as are the Father and the Son (Matthew 28:19. 1 Corinthians 12:4-6. 2 Corinthians 13:14).

2. *He is eternal* (Hebrews 9:14). He did not start to exist at Pentecost, for that event marked the moment when he began to work in a new way. He had been present from the very beginning. He shared in the work of Creation (Genesis 1:2; 2:7). He helped to sustain life on earth (Job 33:4), to empower God's servants for special tasks (Judges 3:10 &c) and to inspire the prophets to proclaim not their own ideas, but the word of God (2 Peter 1:21).

3. *He is moral.* He is the *Holy* Spirit. It is his task to bring home to the unbeliever the fact and the guilt of sin (John 16:8-11). He is grieved (Ephesians 4:30) by the sins of those in whose hearts he lives (1 Corinthians 3:16,17), but if he is allowed to do so, he will continue his work of renewal within (Titus 3:5. Romans 8:11), and gradually produce the fruit of the Spirit mentioned in Galatians 5:22,23.

4. *He is practical.* He is, so to speak, the Executive of the Godhead. He carries out the divine purposes in the hearts and lives of the Christian believers. We have seen some of his activities already, and here are others.

a. *He is the Counsellor (see article)* or Comforter—the one who is called alongside to assist in times of difficulty (Acts 9:31), and who, for example, can help us in our prayers (Romans 8:26), and assure us that we are God's children (Romans 8:16).

b. *He is the Director* who will guide us into all truth (John 16:13), because he is himself 'the Spirit of truth' (John 14:17). We see him at work in this way in Acts 16:7.

c. *He is the Ambassador* who represents and communicates of Christ in the heart of the Christian (John 14:17), reminding us of him (John 14:26; 15:26), making his presence real and enhancing his glory and reputation (John 16:7,14).

d. *He is the Strengthener* who equips God's servants, and empowers them to work for him (Acts 1:8; 6:3 &c); and it is he too who bestows those spiritual gifts upon Christians which are to be used for the building up of the Church as a whole (1 Corinthians 12; 14).

Hope

When the Bible uses this word, it means something quite different from the vague and woolly optimism which we express when we say to someone, 'I hope it won't rain tomorrow'. It means rather what we imply when we say, 'Looking forward to seeing you tomorrow', knowing that there is already good evidence that we shall not be disappointed.

Hope in the Bible sense is 'the earnest expectation' of the mother who is looking forward to the birth of her child (Romans 8:19-25), or the confidence of the yachtsman that at the end of the cable there is the anchor, because he has already felt its pull (Hebrews 6:19).

Just as we need faith for the present, so we need hope for the future, because our salvation (Romans 8:25) and our experience of Christ (1 Corinthians 15:19) are incomplete in this life, and stretch forward for their fulfilment into the unseen; and this hope, which is unshared by those who are without God (Ephesians 2:12), not only fills the Christian with joy and peace (Romans 15:13), but inspires him to holier living.

But what, in the case of the Christian, are the grounds for such confidence? What evidence is there that the anchor is there? There are first of all the promises of God himself (Romans 4:18-21) and the resurrection of Jesus from the dead (1 Peter 1:3); but there is also our experience of the presence and power of Christ—'Christ in you, the hope of glory', as Paul puts it (Colossians 1:27). It is for these reasons that while hope calls for patience (Romans 15:4) and steadfast endurance (1 Thessalonians 1:3), the Christian knows that it will not finally be disappointed (Romans 5:5).

Humility

The Latin word *humus* means 'ground', and the humble man is one who lives, so to speak, 'on the ground floor'. When the word is used literally and refers to poverty or social position, then it is translated 'of low estate', or 'of low degree', reserving the word 'humble' itself for moral and spiritual applications.

In this sense the humble man is one who is not self-important or self-assertive, insisting upon his own rights; on the other hand he does not put on a show of false modesty to impress people (Colossians 2:23), but has a quiet and sober estimate of himself in relation to God and his fellow men (Romans 12:3).

Throughout the Bible humility (and its related virtues such as meekness and lowliness) is commanded (Micah 6:8. 1 Peter 5:5,6), praised (Proverbs 16:19) and rewarded (Proverbs 15:33. 1 Peter 5:6); for it is only the humble man who is fully able to enjoy God's help

(James 4:6), guidance (Psalm 25:9) and rest of heart and mind (Matthew 11:28-30). Perhaps however the chief reason for cultivating and practising this virtue is the fact that it lies right at the very heart of the Godhead. We see it in God's personal interest and involvement in his creation and its welfare (Psalm 113:5-9), rather than a cold, spectator-like indifference. We see it in his willingness to dwell in a 'workman's cottage' of the believer's heart as well as in his own 'stately home' (Isaiah 57:15). We see it most supremely when he came to visit and redeem his people (Luke 1:68), becoming truly man (not an angel), a servant (not a prince), and finally accepting the death of a criminal (not a hero) upon a cross (Philippians 2:5-8). There was perhaps no virtue except love which was more strikingly exhibited in the earthly life of Jesus than his meekness or humility. He was 'meek and lowly in heart' (Matthew 11:29), never seeking his own glory (John 8:50) or using his miraculous powers for his own ends. Small wonder that when Paul wanted to teach his readers the lesson of humility, it was to the 'meekness and gentleness of Christ' that he appealed (2 Corinthians 10:1).

Hypocrisy
The word 'hypocrite' was a Greek word meaning 'actor'. Christ used it figuratively in its modern meaning in his dialogue with the religious leaders of his day, because so often he saw that their outward words and deeds were not matched by inward and spiritual realities (Matthew 23:27,28). They displayed it in their judgement of others (Matthew 7:1-5), their attitude towards himself (Luke 12:56), their sense of moral values (Matthew 23:14,15,24,29) and in their practice of religion (Luke 13:15. Matthew 6:2,5,16).

I

Idolatry

An idol is some form of substitute for God. In the Old Testament it was often a graven or molten image (Exodus 32:4,24) which was intended in some way to represent God, providing a material and local focus for worship; while in the New Testament the term was extended to include everything which usurps the place of God as the object of man's loyalty and worship (Matthew 6:24), from covetousness (Colossians 3:5) to false doctrine (1 John 5:20,21).

The Old Testament is not the story of idol-worshippers who gradually turned to the true God. Idolatry is shown as the falling away from spiritual worship because of moral corruption. The history of Israel must therefore be seen as a battle to preserve the pure worship of the one true, living God in the midst of a world where heathen practices were rife. This was the background against which Moses (Deuteronomy 29:16-18) and the prophets (Isaiah 10:10,11) warned and pleaded with the people to keep the second commandment (Exodus 20:4).

Although the Bible insists that idols have no real existence, power or influence (Isaiah 40:18-20. 1 Corinthians 8:4), and are objects of derision (Psalm 115:4-7), it never suggests that they are harmless, for by associating with them, man is not only dishonouring God, but also exposing himself to contact with the powers of evil and demonic forces (1 Corinthians 10:19,20).

Incarnation

This word does not appear in the Bible, but was coined because it expressed what is stated over and over again in the New Testament, namely that Jesus Christ was God 'manifest in the flesh' (1 Timothy 3:16). The word literally means to embody in flesh.

The fact of the incarnation. Nowhere in the Bible is this stated more clearly or simply than in John 1:14, where we read that 'the Word was made flesh, and dwelt among us'. Jesus Christ was God revealed to us in human form. Just as thoughts, if they are to be communicated, must be clothed in words and deeds, so God, who is pure Spirit (John 4:24), can only be known by his fallen creatures if he himself is revealed in human form (Philippians 2:8). The 'idea' must take 'concrete form' and substance. The 'Author' must become the 'Actor', and take the part of one of his characters.

The purpose of the incarnation. But why did he do it? Not simply to make himself known, for that would have been unnecessary if man had never fallen into sin. The purpose of the incarnation was redemptive. The debt for sin had to be paid by man, but it could only be paid by God, and therefore it was necessary for God to become man that he might save us from the consequences of our rebellion and sin, and restore us to fellowship with himself (Philippians 2:5-10. Colossians 1:13-22). It is important, too, to remember that it is only in the incarnate Son of God that we see man as he is intended to be—the perfect 'finished product'. Through Adam we became 'living souls', capable of ordinary, natural life; but through Christ we can fulfil our real destiny and become spiritual beings (1 Corinthians 15:45). The artist, whose first picture was marred by sin and disobedience, has provided us with another flawless 'Original' of which we are to be copies (Romans 8:29).

The nature of the incarnation. The New Testament does not enter into this in great detail. It deals with facts and not theories, and is content to tell us that 'it is in Christ that the complete being of the Godhead dwells embodied' (Colossians 2:9 NEB). It was only in later years that controversy began to rage about the exact nature of the Person of Christ, and how he could at one and the same time be human and divine.

When someone is showing you his property, he often does so by indicating the boundaries beyond which it does not go. It is a little like that with some of the Christian doctrines, and in some ways the incarnation is more easily defined negatively than positively. Jesus was not half human and half divine, a kind of hybrid creation, like the legendary centaur which was half man and half horse. He was fully God and at the same time fully man. Physically, emotionally and intellectually he was a perfect and complete man, and yet never for one moment did he cease to be completely God.

Nor must we think of him as God masquerading as man, but all the time immune from the trials and troubles which beset mortal human nature. He was not like some grand person who occasionally visits a deprived inner city area, returning to his own splendid and luxurious home after each visit. He really lived there. He shared our human nature. He was tempted, just as we are (Hebrews 4:15), he wept (John 11:35), he rejoiced (John 16:33), he suffered (Matthew 16:21) and he died (Philippians 2:8).

It is equally wrong to think of Jesus as a man promoted to be God, rather in the same way as someone is ennobled for distinguished service, and becomes 'Lord Folkestone' or 'Lord Ramsgate'. At his baptism, Jesus was not being elevated to a kind of peerage, but recognized for what he already was, God's only begotten and well-beloved Son (Matthew 3:16,17), designated as the promised Messiah.

It is not surprising that there should be something mysterious and miraculous about the birth of such a Person—the 'God-Man'—and this is in fact what happened, because while Jesus had a human mother, he did not have a human father. In fact we are told that the part usually played by the father in the conception of a child was made unnecessary because of the operation of God's Holy Spirit (Matthew 1:18-20. Luke 1:26-35). As Paul puts it, 'On the human level he was born of David's stock, but on the level of the spirit—the Holy Spirit—he was declared Son of God ...' (Romans 1:3,4 NEB). In the normal way, of course, a 'Virgin Birth', as it is called, would be dismissed as unthinkable; but for Jesus it is an absolutely consistent beginning to a life which exhibited qualities which on the one hand were perfectly human and on the other hand perfectly divine.

Exactly how these two natures, the divine and the human, were united in one Person, we cannot say. But it is only by believing that Jesus was indeed man, capable of experiencing joy and sorrow, temptation and pain, and that he was equally God in character, authority and power, that we can begin to do justice to the language of the New Testament on this mysterious subject.

Inheritance

In the Old Testament we find the idea of inheritance (which meant possession rather than succession) working in two ways. The Promised Land of Canaan was the inheritance which God's people were to enjoy (Joshua 1:1-9); while they themselves were to be his inheritance, a people for his own personal possession (Deuteronomy 7:6; 32:9), a truth which we find reflected in the parable of the Vineyard, where the heir comes to enjoy the fruit of his inheritance (Mark 12:1-12).

In the New Testament these same two ideas are taken over. Because the Christian is a son of God, and therefore a joint-heir with Christ (Romans 8:17), there is prepared in Heaven 'an eternal inheritance' for him (Hebrews 9:15) which 'nothing can destroy or spoil or wither' (1 Peter 1:4 NEB), and of which the Holy Spirit, living in our hearts, is 'the earnest' (see article) or the title-deed (Ephesians 1:14). There is also a sense in which the Christian Church (the New Testament equivalent of the Children of Israel) is Christ's own inheritance (Ephesians 1:18), chosen and purchased by him to fulfil his purposes in the world (1 Peter 2:9,10).

Iniquity
(See SIN)

Inspiration

The Greek word is 'God-breathed', meaning 'out of his mouth' (Proverbs 2:6) not 'into our mind'. It only appears once in the New Testament where it is applied to the Scriptures, which are said to be given 'by the inspiration of God' (2 Timothy 3:16). This means that the Scriptures are not just man's writings stamped with the approval of God, but the authentic record of his own utterances, and the written revelation of his mind and will.

It is this 'inspiration' which gives the Scriptures their unique character. It accounts for the claims made for them by Jesus himself (Luke 24:44, 45. John 10:35) and his followers (2 Peter 1:20,21); for their power in the lives of those who use them (1 Timothy 3:16. 2 Timothy 3:15); for their internal unity (Luke 24:27,32,44-46); and for their persistent endurance throughout the centuries (Matthew 5:18).

63

J

Jealousy

When God introduced himself to his people as 'a jealous God' (Exodus 20:5), he did not of course mean that he was entertaining any feelings of envy. He meant that, like a loving husband, he was not prepared to share the object of his love with anyone or anything else (Isaiah 54:5. Jeremiah 3:14). He wants them to be his own 'special possession' (Deuteronomy 14:2), and unfaithfulness of any sort must 'rouse his jealousy' (Deuteronomy 32:16 NEB. 1 Corinthians 10:22).

The Christian worker too knows something of this jealousy, as he covets people for God's possession, and cannot bear to see them seduced by Satan (2 Corinthians 11:2,3); but in using the word, Paul is careful to explain that he is really sharing in the 'divine jealousy', lest he should be misunderstood.

Jehovah

(See GOD)

Joy

The Bible makes it clear that God 'richly furnishes us with all things to enjoy' (1 Timothy 6:17), and that the natural world is full of things in which we may legitimately rejoice. There is the joy of youthfulness (Ecclesiastes 11:9) and physical strength (Psalm 19:5). There is joy to be found in prosperity (Ecclesiastes 7:14) and in time of harvest (Isaiah 9:3). There is great joy in happy marriage (Proverbs 5:18), in the birth of a child (John 16:21) and in friendship (1 Samuel 20:41,42). Turning to the more specifically spiritual type of joy, we will look first at the Old Testament. Here we find that sometimes joy was a national experience, as when the people were united in seeking God when David was acclaimed king (1 Chronicles 12:40), or the Temple and the city of Jerusalem were finally restored (Ezra 3:11-13. Nehemiah 12:43); and sometimes a more personal experience, when sins were confessed and forgiven (Psalm 51:12), or when men rejoiced in the discovery of God's salvation (Psalm 9:14), his constant presence (Psalm 16:11) and his word (Jeremiah 15:16). Such people, trusting in the Lord, would constantly 'sing for joy' (Psalm 5:11).

In the Gospels we find that the birth of Jesus (Matthew 2:10. Luke 2:10) and his resurrection (Matthew 28:8) were occasions of special joy; while joy was perhaps one of the most precious gifts he bestowed upon his followers (John 16:22). They were to find it in the fact that their names were written in heaven (Luke 10:20), in suffering persecution for his sake (Luke 6:23), in answered prayer (John 16:24) and in service well done (Matthew 25:21). It is one of the great paradoxes of the Christian Faith that 'the Man of Sorrows' (Isaiah 53.3) is able to impart such unquenchable joy (John 17:13).

When we turn to the later books of the New Testament, we see how this worked out in practice. The early Christians found joy in temptation (James 1:2) and suffering (Acts 13:52), joy in an exhausting life of service (Acts 20:24 AV), in prayer, and in watching the spiritual progress of young Christian converts (Philippians 4:1. 1 Thessalonians 2:19,20. 3 John 4).

But this joy was not a synthetic, artificial product, worked up from within. It was entirely supernatural. It was the fruit of the Spirit (Galatians 5:22), nurtured and cultivated by a deep faith in the unseen presence of Jesus Christ (1 Peter 1:8).

Judgement

Although God himself is sometimes spoken of as the Judge (Hebrews 12:23), it is to Jesus Christ that the special prerogative seems to have been given to execute this judgement upon mankind

65

(John 5:22. Acts 10:42); and while the Bible is not precise in every detail, and does not give us an exact programme of events, it makes it quite clear that 'it is appointed unto men once to die, but after this the judgement' (Hebrews 9:27); and it seems from other parts of the New Testament that there will be three separate kinds of judgement.

1. *The judgement of those who have never heard of Christ.* Here the test appears to be the extent to which men have lived up to the light they have been given (Romans 2:6-8), either through nature (Romans 1:20) and their conscience (Romans 2:14,15), or, in the case of the Jews, through the written Law (Romans 2:12). It is in this way that they reveal how they would have treated Christ if they had had the chance to hear about him (Matthew 25:31-46).

2. *The judgement of those who have heard of Christ.* This time the test will be their personal attitude to himself. Those who have repented (Matthew 11:21-24) and believed in him (John 3:16) will find eternal life (John 5:24); but those who have rejected him 'shall not see life; but the wrath of God abideth on' them (John 3:36). For it is only through faith in Christ that salvation is to be found, and to refuse him is to face condemnation (Romans 8:1).

3. *The judgement of believers.* This time it is not eternal salvation that is at stake, but rather rewards and future opportunities of service (Matthew 25:14-30), and the test will be the faithful way in which the Christian has built upon the foundation of his faith, which is Christ (1 Corinthians 3:11-15).

No treatment of this subject can be complete without reference to the Book of Revelation where, in language which is highly symbolic and figurative, we have a solemn and awe-inspiring account of the final judgement (Revelation 20:11-15). There can be no disguising the majestic authority of the Judge, the personal responsibility of man and the final destiny of eternal happiness or irreparable loss.

Justification

It is interesting to find that the Greek word for 'justify' was used in a court of law for declaring a price to be fair in a contract, and though the English word 'justify' literally means to 'make right', it is never used in this sense in the New Testament, but always to 'reckon' or 'declare right' (Romans 4:1-3). The word 'sanctification' is used to express the other idea of making righteous. 'Justify' is therefore a stronger word than 'pardon' or 'forgive', and introduces us to a deeper aspect of the love of God and the atoning work of Christ; for while the other words are more personal in their application, the word 'justification' has quite distinct legal overtones.

1. *It is necessary.* Sin is not merely a personal matter between me and God, for then perhaps he could forgive me outright; but it is 'transgression', or the infringement of his law (1 John 3:4. Romans 4:15). Sin is a personal matter, but transgression is a legal one. I may forgive the man who has stolen my property, but unless he is legally acquitted in court, he will still be guilty and have to pay the penalty; and it is this more serious aspect of sin which is covered by the word 'justification'. If I am to be right with God and his law, I need somehow to be legally acquitted. It should be obvious too that there is nothing that man himself can do to merit acquittal, because good deeds in the past and good resolutions for the future cannot put me on the right side of the law so far as my present offence is concerned (Romans 3:20).

2. *It is possible.* The only hope for justification lies in the possibility of someone who is in a position to do so offering to accept the penalty on my behalf, and not only doing that, but also in some way clothing me in his own innocence. We cannot imagine or construct a human situation in which such a transaction would be possible, because even if someone were allowed to pay the penalty on my behalf, I should still be left with the guilt. But it was precisely this that Jesus Christ achieved upon the cross.

First, he accepted the punishment of sin instead of me, thus setting me free from the penalty of my own offence by bearing it in my place (Romans 3:25; 5:6,8; 8:32,34. 1 Peter 2:24. Isaiah 53:5,6,10. &c); but secondly, he went even further than this, because, having no sin of his own (1 Peter 2:22), he allowed himself to be 'made sin for us ... that we might be made the righteousness of God in him' (2 Corinthians 5:21). Just as my sin was imputed to him, so his righteousness was imputed to me (Philippians 3:9). Because of Adam's offence, sin was imputed to the whole human race; and in the same way because of the sinlessness of Jesus, righteousness may be imputed to every man (Romans 5:15-21).

Justification then is made possible for two reasons—the grace of God (Romans 3:24) and the death of Christ (Romans 5:9). It was God's part, in his infinite mercy, to plan the bridge by which man could once again gain access to him; and it was the work of Jesus, through his death, to span the gulf, and make a new and living way into God's presence for us (Hebrews 10:19,20).

3. *It is effective.* It is clear from what has been said, that man's only hope of justification lies in his acceptance of what Christ has done, and this is what Paul means when he says, 'a man is justified by faith apart from the deeds of the law' (Romans 3:28; 5:1. Galatians 2:16; 3:11). He must appropriate by faith what Christ has purchased with his blood and God offers in love. In doing so he is released from the penalty of sin and its guilt.

Kingdom of God (Heaven)

It is Matthew who speaks of the 'Kingdom of Heaven', because his readers, being Jews, shrank from uttering the name of God; but to non-Jews the phrase would have been unintelligible, and so Mark and Luke speak of the 'Kingdom of God', but mean precisely the same thing.

Towards the end of the Old Testament, the 'Kingdom' was looked forward to as the great turning point in Jewish history, when God would intervene on behalf of his people, restoring their fortunes and releasing them from the power of their enemies (Zechariah 9:9,10. Malachi 4). In the teaching of John the Baptist it began to assume a more moral character (Matthew 3:1-12); but Jesus changed it even more radically still, for while he taught about the future growth of the Kingdom (Matthew 13:33-43), he also showed that it was a present reality, and existed wherever people submitted to his kingly rule. With his coming, God's invasion of the world had begun, and his power was already beginning to reveal itself in a new way (Luke 11:20). But the Kingdom of God differed from ordinary kingdoms, and from what the Jews expected, in three important ways.

1. *It was spiritual, not political.* 'You cannot tell,' said Jesus, 'by

observation when the Kingdom of God comes' (Luke 17:20 NEB); 'for behold, the Kingdom of God is in the midst of you' (Luke 17:21 RSV). In other words, the Kingdom of God is the sphere of Jesus' authority, and exists wherever his kingship is acknowledged. It is not measured in acres or armies, but 'soul by soul and silently its shining bounds increase', and while its final establishment is still future, it is a present experience in the life of the Christian believer.

2. *It was eternal, not temporal* (John 18:36). The kingdoms of this world rise and fall, but the Kingdom of God, because it is based in heaven and will finally be consummated there (Revelation 11:15), can never fail, but will last for ever (Daniel 2).

3. *It was moral, not material* (Romans 14:17. 1 Corinthians 15:50); for its strength did not lie in its material resources or its standard of living, but in 'justice, peace and joy, inspired by the Holy Spirit' (Romans 14:17 NEB). 'He will save his people from their sins' (Matthew 1:21) and sins are their real enemies.

Knowledge

In Jewish thinking and throughout the Bible knowledge had little to do with intellectual contemplation or philosophical thought (Colossians 2:8. 1 Timothy 6:20), but was always related to experience—the practical identification of one person with the heart, mind and will of another. It is significant, for example, that it is the popular Hebrew word for sexual intercourse (Genesis 4:1. Matthew 1:25); and it is regularly used throughout Scripture to describe man's personal relationship with God (Jeremiah 24:7; 31:34. John 17:3. &c), and also God's with man (Psalm 139).

It follows from this that the opposite of knowledge in the Bible is not so much ignorance as disobedience. Even without the background of the Old Testament, ignorance on the part of the Gentiles was regarded as culpable (Romans 1:18-20), and due, not to lack of illumination, but to moral rebellion and decay (Ephesians 4:17-19).

So far as the Christian is concerned, the knowledge of God through Christ (2 Corinthians 4:6) must continue to be his main ambition (Ephesians 4:13. Philippians 3:10), until the time when 'I shall know, even as I am known' (1 Corinthians 13:12).

70

L

Lamb of God

This description of Jesus, first used by John the Baptist (John 1:29), may have suggested many things to the minds of those who heard it. They would remember the part a lamb played in the deliverance of Isaac (Genesis 22:13), and in their own escape as a nation from Egypt (Exodus 12); John's reference to 'the sins of the world' would have revived pictures of the sin-offering brought to the priest (Leviticus 4:32); and there clearly must have been some who remembered how the Servant of the Lord in Isaiah 53 (who has been identified with Jesus) was compared in his innocence and suffering to a lamb. For all these reasons the comparison was a very popular one among some of the later writers in the New Testament (1 Peter 1:18,19. Revelation 5:6; 7:14; 12:11; 13:8 &c).

Law

It is not always easy to be sure to which part of the Old Testament Law, or to which particular Code, the New Testament is referring when it uses the word; but for practical purposes we may take it to mean the whole system of ethics set out at different times in the Old Testament, the 'mountain peak' being the Ten Commandments (Exodus 20).

71

1. *The function of the Law.* In Old Testament days the Law fulfilled three important functions.

(a) It was our schoolmaster or custodian until the coming of Christ (Galatians 3:24), keeping us in check and exercising some sort of restraint over us.

(b) It emphasised the gravity of sin (Romans 7:13), because although sin existed long before the Law was given, no reckoning of it was kept, for where there is no Law there can be no breach of the Law (Romans 4:15; 5:13). The Law provided a proper framework for judgement.

(c) It follows from this that the Law is God's instrument for bringing home to man the nature of his failure, and his personal responsibility for sin (Romans 3:20; 7:7).

2. *The weakness of the Law.* There is nothing wrong with the Law as such. Paul calls it 'holy, and just, and good' (Romans 7:12,16,22); but its weakness lay in the fact that it was impossible through trying to keep the Law for anyone to be justified in the sight of God (Romans 3:20). Those who are trying to do this are in bondage to the Law, and need to be delivered from its power (Romans 7:6).

3. *The place of the Law.* But the fact that the Law has failed in this respect does not mean that it has been overthrown by faith and rendered null and void—quite the reverse (Romans 3:31). Christ did not come to destroy the Law, but to fulfil it, by giving it a new inner and spiritual dimension (Matthew 5:17). This means that while the Christian no longer tries to keep God's commandments as a way of earning his salvation, he does try to do so as a means of expressing his love and gratitude to God. Not only will he now want to obey the Law out of love for Christ, but he will also find that 'love is the fulfilling of the Law' (Romans 13:10), and that there is not one of the Ten Commandments which he can break without violating the principle of love.

4. *The ritual of the Law.* The Epistle to the Hebrews shows how the sacrifice of Christ upon the cross completed for ever all the sacrifices foreshadowed in the Law, thereby making their continuance unnecessary.

Liberty

In what might be called his 'political manifesto' (Luke 4:18), Jesus promised 'to set at liberty those who are oppressed', as Isaiah 61:1 had foretold, and many of his hearers no doubt looked back to the

72

time when their nation had suffered oppression and captivity in Egypt and in Babylon, and remembered with gratitude how God had released them from bondage (Exodus 3:8. Psalm 126).

But it was not from the domination of Rome that Jesus had come to set them free, but from the spiritual forces by which they were kept prisoner—sin (Matthew 1:21. Romans 6:18), fear (Hebrews 2:15), the Law (Romans 8:2) and death (Romans 8:21. 1 Corinthians 15:54).

1. *Liberty is a gift.* It is offered by Christ (John 8:36) as a result of what he did upon the cross (1 Peter 1:18,19), and is produced in the heart of the Christian by the operation of the Holy Spirit (Romans 8:2), for 'where the Spirit of the Lord is, there is liberty' (2 Corinthians 3:17).

2. *Liberty is a privilege.* This liberty (the liberty of God's children—Romans 8:21) must not be abused or allowed to degenerate into licence and self-indulgence (Galatians 5:13. 1 Peter 2:16), or in any way to cause offence to others (1 Corinthians 9:19; 10:29-33). We are free, but not free to do as we like; 'for "What is freedom?" Rightly understood, a universal licence to be good'. It has been given to us that we may dedicate ourselves wholeheartedly to Christ, putting ourselves voluntarily under his command (Romans 6:18. 1 Corinthians 9:21); just as the Israelites were released that they might belong to God in a special way (Exodus 19:3-6).

3. *Liberty is a responsibility.* Paul found that some of his converts were in danger of losing their new-found liberty, and slipping back, in this case, into outworn rituals and traditions. Liberty must be preserved at all costs, and te arged t emt 'Stand firm, then, and refuee to be tied to the yoke of slavery again' (Galatiane 5:1 NEB).

Life

1. *Natural life.* All natural life is the gift of God. It came from him in the first place (Genesis 2:7. Job 33:4). It is he who sustains it day by day (Daniel 5:23. Acts 17:25,28), prolongs it when he sees fit (Psalm 91:16), and finally in his own time brings it to a close (Job 1:21. Ecclesiastes 12:7). It is for this reason that human life, even from the earliest days (Genesis 4:1-13) had been regarded as so precious, and protected by laws (Exodus 20:13).

2. *Spiritual (or eternal) life.* There are a few places in the Old Testament where something more than physical life seems to be implied (Psalm 16:11. Proverbs 3:18), but it is only in the New

Testament that this truth comes to the fore, and when it does, the writers abandon their usual word for life (*bios*) and use another one instead (*zoe*). The starting-point for a study of this subject is John 1:4 where we read, 'In him (Jesus) was life'. He is the source of this life, and it is only through faith in him that we may possess and enjoy it (John 3:36; 17:3); for 'he who has the Son has life, and he who has not the Son of God has not life' (1 John 5:12). Life of this sort is not just everlasting, stretching on into eternity (see article), but life on a new level of dimension which we can begin to enjoy here and now. Man is regarded as spiritually dead until he is 'quickened' into new life through faith in Christ and by the working of the Holy Spirit (Ephesians 2:1. Romans 8:11).

3. *Resurrection life.* 'Because I live,' said Jesus, 'you will live also' (John 14:19 AV). He has finally overcome death, and those who believe in him will share in his resurrection (1 Corinthians 15:12,20). The exact nature of our resurrection (see article) life is uncertain, but we shall be equipped with a 'spiritual body' (1 Corinthians 15:44) which will be adapted to an entirely new kind of existence.

Light

The very first thing that God created for his creatures was light (Genesis 1:3,4), and from very early days it has been contrasted with darkness (see article), which is a symbol of man's sin, and so of God's displeasure and wrath. We first see this distinction made in his judgement on Pharaoh (Exodus 10:21-23), while in the Book of Revelation it marks the difference between hell (Revelation 16:10) and heaven (Revelation 22:5), and describes the path that leads to them (Proverbs 4:18); and whenever the word 'light' is applied to people or things, it is meant to indicate their pure, beneficent nature.

1. God is light (1 John 1:5), a light which is elsewhere described as 'unapproachable' (1 Timothy 6:16), because it stands for his intense white-hot holiness and purity. And his word is 'a lamp unto our feet and a light unto our path' (Psalm 119:105), for as we read it, 'the unfolding (entrance) of thy words gives light' (Psalm 119:130), and we shall be helped to conduct our lives pleasingly to him.

2. Jesus is 'the light of the world' (John 8:12), because in his light we see light or are 'bathed in light' (Psalm 36:9), and by keeping close to him we will be guided aright. His gospel too is described as

74

'light' (2 Corinthians 4:4), because it leads people out of the darkness of sin and death.

3. Christians are also lights (Matthew 5:14-16), shining in a dark place (Philippians 2:15), as they bear witness to Christ. They are to wear 'the armour of light' (Romans 13:12), and so to live that they are worthy of the title 'Children of light' (Ephesians 5:8).

Longsuffering
(See LOVE)

Love
In the Old Testament the Hebrew word for 'love' covers all our English meanings of that word—sexual, social and spiritual— and was translated into Greek as *agape,* a word which scarcely appears in Classical Greek. Its lack of pagan associations therefore made it the obvious word for the New Testament writers to use for Christian love, thus distinguishing it from sexual love (*eros*) on the one hand and brotherly love or friendliness (*philadelphia*) on the other.

Divine love. Because 'God is love' (1 John 4:8), he must from the very beginning have had an object for his love; and this object was Jesus, who spoke of the love which his Father had for him 'before the foundation of the world' (John 17:24). At the very outset of his earthly ministry he was acclaimed by God as 'My beloved Son' (Matthew 3:17), and God reserved for him a special kind of love worthy of their unique relationship (Ephesians 1:6); while throughout his life God's love for him was, if possible, deepened by his perfect obedience to his Father's will (John 10:17).

God's love for man is implicit in his creation of him, and is fully expressed for the first time in Deuteronomy 4:37-40, where it is applied to his specially chosen people. Throughout the Bible God's love for man is always regarded as perfectly consistent with his discipline (Hebrews 12:5-8), and even with his wrath; for we read, 'In overflowing wrath for a moment I hid my face from you but with everlasting love I will have compassion on you' (Isaiah 54.8).

As the Old Testament proceeds, we find God's love compared to that of a father (Psalm 103:13. Malachi 3:17), a mother (Isaiah 49:15; 66:13) and a husband (Hosea 2:19-3:1); and perhaps the most remarkable part of this love is that it is still bestowed, as some of these passages show, on the wayward and the unfaithful. It is 'an everlasting love' (Jeremiah 31:3).

75

When we reach the New Testament, God's love finds its fullest and deepest expression in the gift of his Son to be the Saviour of mankind (John 3:16. Romans 5:8. 1 John 4:10 &c) and in his adoption of us into his family (1 John 3:1). But chiefly of course God's love in the New Testament is continued and fulfilled in the life and work of Jesus himself—'As the Father hath loved me, so have I loved you' (John 15:9). This love, seen all through his earthly ministry, when he was frequently 'moved with compassion' by human suffering and need (Matthew 9:36. Luke 7:13), reached its climax in his death upon the cross (Galatians 2:20), but still continues to surround and protect all who belong to him by faith (Romans 8:35). Not only this, but his love for us is to be the example of our love for others (Ephesians 5:2. John 13:34), and the inspiration of our service for him (2 Corinthians 5:14).

Human love. Man's love for God is not original, but derived. It is only because he has first loved us, that we are capable of loving him in return (1 John 4:19). From the earliest days love is put before man as his most important duty to God (Deuteronomy 6:5). Because it is commanded, it is primarily a matter of the will rather than the feelings, and means that the whole personality ('heart ... and soul ... and might') is to be directed towards God, pleasing him and serving him; and almost invariably throughout the Bible we find that obedience is the result and the proof of love (Deuteronomy 10:12. John 14:15; 15:14. 1 John 5:3).

No one can truthfully say that he loves God if at the same time he hates his fellow-men (1 John 4:20), and love towards them is one of the hall-marks of the real Christian (John 13:35). It is a love which must be displayed not only to friends (John 15:13), but to the ordinary people whom we call neighbours (Mark 12:31) and even towards enemies (Matthew 5:44); but perhaps it is reserved in a unique way for those with whom we share our faith in Jesus Christ (John 13:35). This special form of 'brotherly love' is something which should spring up quite naturally between Christians (1 Thessalonians 4:9), but it needs to be fostered and even incited or 'provoked' (Hebrews 10:24). This love for fellow-Christians will show itself in service (Galatians 5:13), generosity (1 Peter 3:8,9), suffering (2 Corinthians 12:15) and humility (Romans 12:10); while for a complete analysis of it, we need to turn to 1 Corinthians 13.

M

Man

'What is man?' asks the psalmist (Psalm 8:4), and while the Bible does not provide us with a complete scientific answer to that question, it does reveal some of the most fundamental and important things about him and shows him to be what Pascal has called 'the glory and the scandal of the universe'.

1. *Man created.* First of all the Bible makes it quite clear that man occupies a very special place in the universe (Genesis 1:26-28), and was the climax of God's creative activity. He was made to control and subdue nature (Psalm 8:6-8) and also that he might enjoy a special relationship with his Maker, and bring glory to his name (Isaiah 43:7,21). It was in order to make this relationship possible that man was made 'in the image of God' (Genesis 1:26,27). This clearly had nothing to do with his physical appearance, for in this respect he was in many ways 'like the beasts that perish' (Psalm 49:12. Ecclesiastes 3:19). It consisted rather in the possession of those faculties which made him capable of communion with God and obedience to his will, and of a character with the potential to reflect perfectly the splendour of God's holiness and power. In other words, unlike even the highest animals, man is a rational, moral, responsible and spiritual being.

77

It is difficult and perhaps impossible to reach any final understanding of the structure of man from what we read in the Bible. Words like 'body', 'soul' and 'spirit' are not precisely defined, and the matter is confused still further by another group of words like 'mind', 'conscience' and 'heart' which are used to describe parts of him or some of his activities. Perhaps we are safe in saying that 'soul' usually means the whole man, including body and mind, or what we would call the personality; and 'spirit' is that part of him which is capable of responding to God (John 4:23). In other words, we can say that man is a soul, but has a spirit. The word 'heart' (see article), while occasionally used to describe the seat of the emotions (2 Samuel 14:1), more usually corresponds to the word 'soul', and sometimes (together with mind, conscience and spirit) constitutes what Paul calls 'the inward man' (2 Corinthians 4:16 AV) as distinct from 'the outward man' or body. It is tempting to try to make a neat definition of man into three or four tiers, rather like self-contained flats, the body being on the ground floor and the spirit on the top; but the Bible simply will not lend itself to such a construction. It depicts man as being more like a large, rambling country house, where you never quite know which floor you are on, where rooms open unexpectedly into each other, and where, if you approach a room from one direction you call it the 'Hall', and from another the 'Drawing-room'.

2. *Man disgraced.* The Bible teaches us that man is a fallen being, and traces this calamity back to his act of disobedience in the Garden (Genesis 3). As a result of this the image was damaged (Romans 3:23), but not completely destroyed (1 Corinthians 11:7. James 3:9), and the special relationship broken (Genesis 3:22-24. Isaiah 59:1,2). Through one man's disobedience, sin, with its disastrous consequences, passed into the human race, so that everyone born into the world is tainted with its poison (Psalm 51:5. Romans 5:14-19) and liable to God's judgement.

3. *Man redeemed.* The whole Bible can be read as the story of man's redemption. There was the Law, through which came the knowledge of sin (Romans 3:20). There was the whole system of typology, beginning with the Flood (Genesis 6) and continuing with the animal sacrifices by means of which man was taught that his redemption depended upon the grace of God. And there was the challenge of the prophets, calling people back to repentance (Isaiah 1:18 &c).

It is in the Person and work of Christ that all these three converge into fulfilment. He embodied the Law in his perfect life. Then he offered that life as a sacrifice for sin. Finally, he invited people to 'believe in him' that they might share in his gift of everlasting life. It is in response to this call that man is redeemed and restored.

But while man may once again enjoy unbroken friendship with God (1 Peter 3:18), the restoration is not yet complete, nor the effects of the Fall entirely undone. Evil has not been eradicated from the world, and the New Testament employs the word 'flesh' (see article) to describe its continued presence in human nature. The country has, so to speak, been reoccupied by the rightful King, and the enemy driven underground. But the enemy is still active, there are many pockets of resistance, and the day of his total elimination is yet to come.

It appears from Romans 8:19-23 that the whole creation was in some way affected by the Fall of man, and eagerly awaits the day of final victory which will usher in what is called 'the glorious liberty of the children of God'. That day will come with the return of Christ, and the overthrow of Satan; and once again the image of God in man will be fully and perfectly restored (Romans 8:29. 1 Corinthians 15:49. 1 John 3:2).

Mediator

'There is no umpire between us', says Job, when protesting his innocence before God (Job 9:33), and anxious to convince him. In the same verse the NEB speaks of 'arbitration', and both words express very aptly what we mean by a 'mediator'. He is literally 'a middle man', and it is his task to come between two people for the purpose of reconciling them, and the only 'umpire' between God and man is Jesus Christ (1 Timothy 2:5). Through his death he removed the enmity between us, and built a bridge of reconciliation (Colossians 1:20. Hebrews 9:24). The state of war is over, and there is peace with God through our Lord Jesus Christ (Romans 5:1. Ephesians 2:12-17).

But there is a sense in which the mediation of Christ is continuous; for it is only through him that we can offer our prayers, worship and service to God (John 14:14. Hebrews 13:15), and ask forgiveness for our sins (1 John 2:1. Hebrews 7:25). It is only in him that we are acceptable to God (Ephesians 1:6), because God is able to look upon us only in and through his Son.

Meekness
(See HUMILITY)

Mercy

Like grace (see article), mercy only operates in one direction, from the strong to the weak, or from the rich to the poor. In the Old Testament it also denotes God's loyalty to his covenant with his people, and is sometimes rendered 'steadfast love' (Psalm 100:5 RSV), because he will not abandon them, despite their unfaithfulness. In the New Testament its meaning is much the same as that of grace, but it suggests love or pity directed to man in a state of misery (Matthew 5:7. Luke 17:13; 18:13) rather than in one of guilt.

Ministry

This word is used today to describe a collection of people engaged in one particular form of service. Thus we talk about 'The Ministry of Agriculture', and the Oxford Dictionary, when applying it to the Christian Church, gives 'The Clerical Profession' as a definition. In New Testament days, however, the word had not yet acquired this specialised meaning, and was used to describe the work itself.

The 'ministry' therefore was any form of Christian service, and those who took part in it were 'ministers' (1 Corinthians 3:5) or 'servants', but quite early on it came to be applied chiefly to work of the more spiritual nature, as distinct from the secular duties which had to be performed (Acts 6:1-5) and for which a special group of men who were not apostles were recruited.

We read of 'the ministry of the word' (Acts 6:4) which meant the expounding and explaining of the Scriptures which we find Paul doing at Thessalonica (Acts 17:2), and Apollos with great effect at Corinth (Acts 18:28); and we also read of 'the ministry (or service—NEB) of reconciliation' (2 Corinthians 5:18,19), which meant offering Christ to people as the one who had died to reconcile man to God (Colossians 1:20).

There was great diversity among the ministers. Some were apostles, some prophets, evangelists, pastors and teachers (Ephesians 4:11); while others were endowed with the gift of healing, performing miracles or speaking in tongues (1 Corinthians 12:28). But this diversity had but a single aim; equipping Christians to play their part in building up the Church into a united body of believers (Ephesians 4:1-13).

The great variety of gifts and functions which God has distributed throughout the Church have been given so that it may minister as a whole, and not just as a collection of individuals. It is like the body, every single limb and organ of which must exercise its particular function if the purpose of its existence is to be fulfilled (1 Corinthians 12:7,12. Ephesiane4:15,16).

Miracles

Miracles are often thought to be contrary to nature, but it would be more accurate to say that they are contrary to what is known of the laws of nature. From our finite point of view they may look like interruptions in the inevitable process of nature, whereas they are in fact happening according to higher laws known only to God himself.

What, to a horse or dog, is a supernatural interference in its affairs on the part of man would, if it had the mind of man, be seen as perfectly normal human activity. In the same way it ought not to surprise us if natural processes are interrupted, altered or reversed in accordance with God's divine will and purpose.

The Bible records many such miracles, and though perhaps in some cases there may have been a natural explanation (eg Joshua 3:16) the supernatural alone can account for the prediction, timing and incidence of the particular event.

The greatest of all the miracles—what C. S. Lewis called 'The Grand Miracle'—was of course the resurrection (see article) of Jesus from the dead. All who have studied this subject open-mindedly agree that it is perhaps the best attested of all the miracles, and if it is true, then it makes all the others look almost trivial by comparison. 'If God can do this,' we find ourselves saying, 'then he can do anything.'

When we turn to the purpose of the miracles, the Bible seems to suggest four reasons why they were performed.

1. *To reveal God's power* (Psalm 145:3-6). It was through his 'great wonders' (Psalm 72:18; 136:4) that God was able to distinguish himself from the local 'gods', and reveal himself as the one, true, living God; a fact which it was hoped would in due course impress itself upon the heathen (Ezekiel 39:21-24).

2. *To benefit God's people.* From the very earliest days, and right through the New Testament, this was the case. Miracles were never performed for their own sake, but they always had a purpose which was beneficial to the people of God. There were miracles at critical periods of history: the Exodus, the entry into Canaan, and during the period of apostasy when Elijah and Elisha kept alive the flame

of true, spiritual religion; and in the New Testament, we find miracles attending the birth and resurrection of Jesus. On a humbler level too, miracles always brought a personal or social benefit—relieving pain and suffering, saving life, casting out demons, and so on.

3. *To confirm the faith of believers.* Miracles were rarely if ever performed to convince the sceptic. The man who would not believe the spoken word would not respond even if it were supported by some miracle performed for his benefit. We see this clearly in the answer that was given to Dives (Luke 16:31). The reason may have been partly that there were false wonder-workers in the world (Deuteronomy 13:2,3. Matthew 7:22; 24:24), and miracles in themselves did not guarantee the authenticity of the spoken word. On the other hand, miracles did serve a very important purpose in strengthening the faith of those who already believed (Exodus 14:31) or were inclined to do so. It was after the miracle at Cana, for example, that we read 'his disciples believed on him' (John 2:11); while in John 4 the healing of the nobleman's son gave new confidence to the faith which his father already possessed (John 4:50,53), rather as the 'Confirmatory Copy' of a telegram will establish beyond doubt what has already been related over the telephone.

4. *To teach a hidden lesson.* This was especially true of the miracles of Jesus which were often referred to as 'signs', (John 2:11). This means that there was an inner spiritual meaning which he was anxious for those who witnessed them to understand. The turning of the water into wine, for example, was followed by Christ's teaching on the new birth (John 3); the 'Feeding of the Five Thousand' by that about 'the Bread of Life' (John 6:35); while the last of his great miracles, the raising of Lazarus (John 11) foreshadowed his own resurrection from the dead.

Mystery

This is a fascinating word. It comes from the Greek *musterion*, and is related to the verb *muo*, which means to close the eyes or lips (hence 'mute'). In pagan religion it meant a secret or a secret doctrine known only to the initiated, but in the New Testament sense it is a secret which God wants to make known and has charged his servants to declare to all who have ears to hear. For this reason the NEB has generally abandoned the translation 'mystery', favoured by the AV and sometimes the RSV as well, because this word suggests an insoluble problem or undiscoverable truth. It prefers instead the word 'secret', but we must remember that it is an 'open secret' which God is anxious for all of us to share.

It is applied in the New Testament to the whole range of spiritual truth which, to those with eyes to see, was revealed in the coming, the Person and the work of Jesus Christ. Thus Jesus himself spoke of 'the mysteries (secrets—NEB) of the kingdom of God' (Luke 8:10), and Paul wrote, 'Great indeed, we confess, is the mystery of our religion ...' (1 Timothy 3:16).

More particularly it was applied to the gospel (Ephesians 6:19) which 'for long ages' had been kept a secret (Romans 16:25), but was now made known in Christ (Colossians 1:26,27); the intimate relationship between Christ and his Church (Ephesians 5:32); and the nature of our resurrection existence (1 Corinthians 15:51).

These were some of the aspects of 'God's mystery' (Colossians 2:2) of which Paul and others regarded themselves as stewards (1 Corinthians 4:1). It is not given to everyone to understand or grasp these mysteries, and although it was Paul's responsibility, and that of every Christian, to try 'to make all men see what is the plan of the mystery' (Ephesians 3:9), such things are only 'spiritually discerned' (1 Corinthians 2:14) and not understood by the ordinary, unaided human mind (Matthew 16:13-17). Just as infra-red rays, for example, cannot be detected without the help of a scientific device, so these mysteries can be discerned only through the eye of humble and obedient faith.

N

Name

Names in the Bible served four purposes.

1. *To identify.* This was their simplest and most obvious use, and perhaps their only one in England today; for a name is a personal label used to identify something or someone. We are told, for example, that Adam named the animals, and that they went by those names thereafter (Genesis 2:19-20).

2. *To signify.* Much more importantly, when a name was given to someone in the Bible, it was nearly always associated with some experience or event of great significance. Abraham's new name indicated the part he was to play as the father of a nation (Genesis 17:5,6); Jacob's marked a turning point in his life (Genesis 32:28), and so did Simon's (John 1:42); while the name 'Jesus' signified the work he had come to do (Matthew 1:21).

3. *To typify.* In a metaphorical sense the 'name' of someone often represents or stands for his person or character. It could imply dignity (Philippians 2:9,10), as when we say, 'He has made a great name for himself', authority (John 14:14), as when we say, 'Please use my name', and integrity (Psalm 8:9 AV), as, for example, when we say 'This firm has an excellent name'. It was because of all that it stood for, that the Third Commandment forbids us to take the

name of God in vain (Exodus 20:7); for to use it in a cheap or empty way is to denigrate what it represents, namely his perfect character of holiness, love and power.

4. *To unify*. When a woman marries, she loses her own surname and takes that of her husband, and this is a sign of a new relationship between them (Isaiah 4:1); and it is interesting to notice that God's people are 'called by the name of the Lord' (Deuteronomy 28:9,10. Numbers 6:27. Isaiah 43:7). Christians bear the name of Christ, an honour of which they must be worthy (2 Timothy 2:19) and for which they must be prepared to suffer (1 Peter 4:14).

Obedience

The first thing the Bible makes clear on this subject is that God, by virtue of his position as Sovereign Creator, has a perfect right to ask for the obedience of his creatures. It was 'the LORD God' who commanded Adam not to eat the fruit in the garden (Genesis 2:16,17), and when introducing the Ten Commandments he began by saying, 'I am the LORD your God ...' (Exodus 20:2).

We notice next that he has not left us in any doubt as to what his commandments (see article) are. We can find them throughout the Bible, and ignorance is no excuse, because we are told to 'seek for all the commandments of the Lord your God' (1 Chronicles 28:8). As we do so, we shall find that they cover not only our moral behaviour, but that obedience to God will also mean a willing response to the gospel (Romans 6:17), involving repentance from sin (1 Peter 1:14) and faith in Jesus Christ (Acts 6:7). There are, too, those personal occasions when God speaks individually to one of his servants in their heart and conscience (Isaiah 30:21), and when he expects the same sort of obedience that he had from Abraham (Hebrews 11:8).

Jesus himself provides the perfect example of obedience from the earliest days when he was 'about his Father's business' (Luke 2:49

AV), and his food was to do the will of his Father (John 4:34) until we read that he 'became obedient unto death, even the death on a cross' (Hebrews 5:8. Philippians 2:8). Love was his motive for obedience, and it is to be ours as well. If we love him we shall keep his commandments (John 14:15. 1 John 5:3), and we are his 'friends' if we do whatever he commands us (John 15:14).

Finally, we must notice that from the very earliest days obedience has been the secret of blessing—personal or national, material or spiritual; and there is this constantly recurring refrain attached to God's demand for obedience—'that it may go well with thee ...' (Deuteronomy 4:40).

P

Parables

A parable (the word means 'to lay one thing alongside another' and, therefore, to make a comparison) was the word used in the New Testament to describe stories which Jesus told, and covered everything from a simple metaphor or simile (Mark 13:28) to an elaborate and almost allegorical story like that of the Prodigal Son (Luke 15) or the Sower and the Seed (Matthew 13).

Two mistakes must be avoided in studying the parables. First, they are usually intended to teach a few main lessons, and attempts to fasten meanings on to every detail are bound to fail. Secondly, moral issues which are irrelevant to the story should be ignored. For example, the fact that the Unjust Steward was commended for his wisdom does not mean that his behaviour was morally justifiable (Luke 16:1-9), any more than Jesus was commending theft when he compared his return to a thief coming in the night (Matthew 24:42-44).

The purpose of the parables was to make truth understandable and memorable by translating it into the language and experience of everyday life. The method is the greatest single feature of the teaching of Jesus, and we read that 'he said nothing to them without a parable' (Matthew 13:34).

People have been puzzled by a passage like Mark 4:11,12 where it seems that the purpose of the parable was the exact opposite of that stated above, and was intended to conceal rather than reveal the truth. The probable answer is that Jesus was describing the effect of the parables on those who were spiritually blind to their meaning; for in Hebrew thought the final result of something was often expressed as if it had been an original intention (Isaiah 6:9,10). But on the other hand there may have been occasions when more direct teaching would have enabled the authorities to 'take hold of what he said' (Luke 20:20), and threaten the close of his ministry before the time. The parables may therefore have provided a kind of 'code' between himself and his sympathizers.

Paradise

The word, originally Persian, means 'a walled garden', and in the three places where it is used in the New Testament it indicates the place where souls go immediately after death (Luke 23:43). It is difficult to be more precise than this, and to say whether Jesus, Paul (2 Corinthians 12:3) and John (Revelation 2:7) were describing exactly the same place, and whether it was synonymous with Heaven. People often speak of 'England' when they mean 'Great Britain', and the distant foreigner is satisfied. It could be that the relationship between 'Paradise' and 'Heaven' is of the same kind. (See also under HELL).

Patience

The root idea of this word in Hebrew is 'long' or 'slow' and in Greek it has the thought of endurance. It shows itself in God's nature in such phrases as 'long-suffering' (Psalm 86:15 AV) or 'slow to anger'. 'The God of patience' as he has been called (Romans 15:5) shows this attitude towards mankind in his reluctance to judge them (1 Peter 3:20) and in the time he allows for men everywhere to repent (Romans 9:22. 2 Peter 3:9).
So far as Christians are concerned, this divine quality of patience must be reflected in their attitude towards other people (1 Thessalonians 5:14) and towards situations. The Christian needs patience to run the race that is set before him (Hebrews 12:1,2), to face temptation (James 1:3,4) and persecution (1 Peter 2:20). He needs it also to inherit the promises of Christ (Hebrews 10:36), and perhaps especially the promise of his Second Coming (James 5:7,8). It will be noticed that other versions than the AV tend to favour words like 'perseverance', 'resolution', and 'steadfastness'

because patience is not just waiting for things to happen in a negative way, but actively and positively preparing ourselves to meet them.

Peace

The word (*shalom* in Hebrew and *eirene* in Greek) means completeness or harmony, such as when a number of musical instruments are playing together in an orchestra. It describes the state of affairs that existed before the world was dislocated by sin and will again exist after sin is finally exterminated (Isaiah 55:12). God himself is the source of peace. Several times he is by Christians described as 'the God of peace' (Romans 15:33 &c), while the title 'Prince of Peace' (Isaiah 9:6) is rightly ascribed by Christians to Jesus; and he wants his people to enjoy this peace—the peace of a 'river' (Isaiah 48:18) compared with the restlessness of a 'troubled sea' (Isaiah 57:20,21).

1. *Peace with God.* The Bible shows us that God and man are at enmity and war with each other (Romans 5:10), and that Jesus came that through his death he might reconcile us to God, so making peace (Colossians 1:20. Romans 5:1).

2. *Peace of God.* Once the rebels have surrendered and made peace with God, they may enjoy the peace *of* God ruling as Sovereign in their hearts and minds. (Compare 'Pax Romana' or 'Pax Britannica'). It comes through faith in his presence and power (Isaiah 26:3), through a study of his word and promises (Psalm 119:165) and through prayer (Philippians 4:6,7); and it 'garrisons' the heart against fear and anxiety.

3. *Peace on earth.* It follows that all who serve the Prince of Peace should enjoy peace among themselves, and they are encouraged in the Bible to do all they can to 'seek peace and pursue it' (1 Peter 3:11. 2 Timothy 2:22) and to preserve it (Ephesians 4:3). But while peace among Christians is a natural and proper outcome of their relationship to Christ, they are also as far as possible to live peaceably with all men (Romans 12:18), and to remember the special blessing that Jesus promised to the 'peace-makers' (Matthew 5:9).

Pledge

(See GUARANTEE)

Power

The Greek word here is *dunamis* (from which we get our word

90

'dynamite'), and was used to describe a person's capacity to do something and often to afford something financially—e.g. 'according to his means' (2 Corinthians 8:3).

1. *The Power of God.* God is the Source of all power, for we read that 'power belongs to God' (Psalm 62:11. 1 Chronicles 29:11,12). It is seen in his creation—'in his mighty firmament' (Psalm 150:1), in the way he sustains the universe and all that is in it (Psalm 65:5-8) and in his mighty acts on behalf of mankind (Psalm 111:6). It is seen in the life of Jesus, and supremely in his resurrection (Romans 1:4. Ephesians 1:19,20), in the power of the gospel to save men and women (Romans 1:16), and in his ability to keep and uphold all who rely upon him in faith (1 Peter 1:5). Such power as man enjoys over the created world (Genesis 1:26-28) is derived entirely from God himself (Psalm 68:35).

2. *The power of Christ.* Another Greek word ('authority', see article) is used to describe the power of Jesus when it refers to the effect of his teaching (Matthew 7:29), his right to forgive sins (Matthew 9:6) and to commission his disciples (Matthew 28:18-20); but it is power of the dynamic sort, or 'might', which is expressed in his miracles (Luke 5:17), will one day attend his return in glory (Luke 21:27) and is exercised on behalf of Christians at all times (2 Corinthians 12:9).

3. *The power of the Holy Spirit.* The coming of the Holy Spirit at Pentecost meant that the power of God was harnessed to the life of the Christian believer in a new way (Acts 1:8; 2:1-3). It enabled the disciples to perform miracles (Acts 3:12), to witness for Christ in a courageous and effective way (Acts 4:33), and to maintain an inner spiritual life of tranquillity and strength (Ephesians 3:16).

Praise

'Making a noise' is the idea behind the Hebrew word for 'praise' (*halal*), and it is interesting to see how often in the Old Testament God's people are encouraged to do this as an act of thanksgiving to him (Psalm 66:1; 95:1; 111-113). They are to praise him for the fact of their creation (Psalm 139:13-18), for the way he answers their prayers (Psalm 118:21) and for all the marvellous things that he has done for them in the world (Psalm 111). We find too that not only people (Psalm 113:1), but nature (Psalm 148:3,4) and every kind of musical instrument (Psalm 150:3-5) are enlisted into this 'Hallelujah Chorus'.

In the New Testament the English word 'praise' appears less often, though its related words such as 'thanksgiving' and 'bless' frequently occur. But we find it mentioned on certain important occasions. There was an outburst of praise following the birth of Jesus (Luke 2:13,20), another as the disciples began to live in the experience of the resurrection (Luke 24:53), and a third when the Holy Spirit was given, and began to manifest his power in the early Christian Church (Acts 2:47); and all aspects of true praise are found in heaven (Revelation 4 and 5).

From the very earliest days of the Christian Church praise has often expressed itself in song, and it is interesting to notice the references to this practice in the New Testament. Paul speaks of 'psalms and hymns and spiritual songs' (Ephesians 5:19), and it was no doubt some of these that he and Silas used in the Philippian jail to the astonishment of the other prisoners (Acts 16:25); for singing is not only the sign of a merry and grateful heart (James 5:13), but also the cure for one which is threatened by anxiety or fear.

If there is a distinction between praise and thanksgiving, it could perhaps be said that we praise God for what he is and we thank him for what he does; but often, particularly in the Old Testament, the two converge and overlap.

Prayer

In the Bible prayer is a kind of 'portmanteau' word, and includes all the attitudes of the human spirit in its approach to God. This means that adoration (Revelation 1:12-18) is an essential part of prayer, and so are confession (Psalm 51), praise (Psalm 103), thanksgiving (Luke 17:11-19), petition (2 Samuel 7:18-25; 1 Samuel 1:9-11), intercession (Genesis 18:23-33; Numbers 21:7) and communion (Luke 10:39).

Many of the above often form part of a continuous time of prayer, but there are also instances of ejaculatory prayer at some moment of crisis. Nehemiah used this method when a quick decision was necessary (Nehemiah 2:1-5) and Simon Peter in a moment of physical danger (Matthew 14:28-33). We notice too that there were times when one person would lead a congregation in prayer (1 Chronicles 16) to which 'all the people said Amen' (1 Chronicles 16:1-36); and when a small group would meet together to pray for some special need or problem (Daniel 2:14-18. Acts 12:5. Matthew 18:20).

Prayer is represented in the Bible as one of man's primary duties. We are told that men 'ought always to pray' (Luke 18:1 AV, RSV) and to 'pray without ceasing' (1 Thessalonians 5:17 AV); and it was to encourage us to pray that Jesus himself provided us with a pattern and even a framework for prayer which we call 'The Lord's Prayer', and taught us to think of God as a Father who is more ready to hear than we are to ask (Luke 11:1-13).

Certain careful conditions are attached to prayer if it is to be answered. There must be no sin harboured in our hearts and minds (Psalm 66:18). We must have steadfast faith in God's power to give us what we ask (James 1:5,6; 5:15), but it must be in the name of Christ (John 14:14), and it must be according to the will of God (1 John 5:14). This last condition may account for the fact that if a prayer is not granted. God, having some better plan for us, will often answer it in another way (2 Corinthians 12:8,9).

The Bible nowhere suggests that prayer is a natural human exercise. It is the Holy Spirit who plants the desire in our hearts, gives us the strength to pray as we should and makes our prayers acceptable to God (Romans 8:26-27). This is what Paul meant by praying in 'the power of the Spirit' (Ephesians 6:18 NEB), and Jude also (Jude 20). Just as the natural man cannot receive spiritual things (1 Corinthians 2:14), so neither can we pray acceptably to God. Acceptable prayer begins with God and makes its way back to him through the work of the Holy Spirit in the heart of the believer.

Finally we must remember that it is only for the sake of Christ that God can receive our prayers; for but for his death upon the cross, sinful man could have no right of access into the presence of a holy God (Ephesians 2:18. Hebrews 9:19-22).

Preaching

(See also GOSPEL)

To preach is to announce good news, and the word (*euangelizo*) is applied in Greek history to the announcement of a military victory and even of someone's engagement to be married. There are several other Greek words which the AV translates as 'preach', but *euangelizo* is regularly translated by AV and RSV as 'preach the gospel', or good news.

The English word has a clear connexion with the prophecy of Old Testament days, and both Noah (2 Peter 2:5) and Jonah (Jonah 3:2) are spoken of as preaching, but it only reaches its full meaning in the New Testament with the announcement that Jesus Christ has come into the world as the Saviour of mankind (Luke 2:10).

93

There are other ways in which the truths of the Christian faith can be communicated, and we read of Paul 'arguing' (Acts 17:2), 'talking' (Acts 20:7), 'testifying' (Acts 28:23) and 'teaching' (Acts 20:20). But the gospel is News, and if it has not been heard before, then before any of these other methods can be used, it must be preached, though this does not necessarily mean a formal sermon, and is often a simple statement made by one person to another. It is because the gospel cannot be heard 'without a preacher' (Romans 10:14) that communicating the gospel is the most important task of the Christian, dwarfing everything else he does (1 Corinthians 9:16); and in fact when some of Paul's enemies took advantage of his imprisonment to preach the gospel in a way he did not approve, we find him actually rejoicing that, however deficiently, the message was being proclaimed (Philippians 1:14-18).

Finally, the would-be preacher must be commissioned by God for his task (Romans 10:15), he must be convinced of the unique and incorruptible value of his message (Galatians 1:6-9), and he must be prepared to be thought 'foolish' by those who think that truth can only be reached by intellectual argument and discussion (1 Corinthians:17-21).

Predestination
(See ELECTION)

Pride
Pride is perhaps the basic human sin, because it was man's original desire to be like God and to share his knowledge (Genesis 3:5,6) that led to his disobedience and downfall; and human pride in its turn may perhaps be traced back to Satan's own attempt to usurp the sovereignty of God (Isaiah 14:12-14).

Throughout the Bible therefore pride is condemned as hateful to God (Proverbs 16:5). It is because of his pride that man will not naturally seek after God (Psalm 10:4), and it is what makes our own good works unacceptable to him (Ephesians 2:8-10) as a way of earning our salvation. Pride begins in the heart (Proverbs 16:5. Mark 7:21), but often spreads to a man's looks (Proverbs 6:17), words (Psalm 12:3) and deeds (Psalm 31:23), and it frequently leads to strife (Psalm 140:5), deceit (Psalm 31:18) and cruelty (Zechariah 9:6,7).

God can have nothing to do with the proud man. He knows him

'afar off' (Psalm 138:6), and will frequently allow his downfall (Proverbs 16:18); for it is only the humble whom he is able to forgive and to help (James 4:6), and in due time to satisfy and exalt (Luke 1:51-53). The perfect example of humility is of course Jesus himself, and it is interesting to study how he was willing to come down the same ladder that man in his pride had from the earliest days tried to climb (Genesis 11:1-8. Philippians 2:5-8).

Priest

In the Old Testament there were two people who stood between God and man — the Prophet and the Priest. The prophet (see article) was God's ambassador to man, proclaiming the divine will and purpose; while the priest was man's ambassador to God, representing the people, and making sacrifice for their sins.
In the patriarchal times the head of the family fulfilled this function, and offered the sacrifices (Genesis 8:20; 31.54. Job 1:5); but under the Law, Aaron and his descendants were appointed priests (Exodus 28), and were specially set apart for this purpose.
When we come to the New Testament, we find that Jesus Christ was both prophet and priest. As prophet, he proclaimed God's will to the people; and as priest he offered himself as the final sacrifice for the sins of the world; and because the sacrifice he made was 'full, perfect and sufficient', he can have no successor, and it need never be repeated. This is the theme of Hebrews 7-10.
The word 'priest', in this sacrificing sense (*hiereus*) is never applied specifically to the Christian minister, although all Christians are described as kings and priests (Revelation 1:6. 1 Peter 2:5,9), because they offer spiritual sacrifices to God in the form of praise, thanksgiving and service (See SACRIFICE).
The English word 'priest' is derived from *presbyter* or elder (see article), and the English reformers used it in this sense, and not as the equivalent of *hiereus*, as the official Latin translation of the Anglican Book of Common Prayer shows.

Promise

A promise is an assurance given by one person to another that something will or will not take place according to his word. In the Bible there are a great many promises given us by God, some of which have been fulfilled already, many of which the Christian can enjoy today in his own experience, and some of which have still to come to pass. In one or two cases God confirmed his promise with an oath (Hebrews 6:13-18), as though to take account of the frailty of human faith; and in a great many cases the promises are conditional upon some act of obedience on our part—'Trust in the Lord and do good; so you will dwell in the land and enjoy security' (Psalm 37:3), is but one example of hundreds.

When anyone makes a promise, two questions always arise: Will he keep his word? Can he do so? In other words, the fulfilment of a promise always depends upon the integrity and the ability of the person who makes it.

When God promises we may have perfect confidence in his integrity. Those who have put him to the test will declare, 'Great is thy faithfulness' (Lamentations 3:23 AV, RSV), while the Psalmist tells us that 'His faithfulness reaches unto the clouds' (Psalm 36:5) ('to the skies'—NEB). He who has called us can be counted upon to see us through (1 Thessalonians 5:24), to forgive us when necessary (1 John 1:9) and to keep us true to himself (1 Peter 4:19). Even 'if we are faithless, he remains faithful for he cannot deny himself' (2 Timothy 2:13).

We may also have complete confidence in his ability. He is in sovereign control of his universe, and he is able to do what he has promised (Romans 4:21); and when perhaps the fulfilment of his promise lies in the future, he often gives us a foretaste of the blessing to come—the presence of his Holy Spirit in our hearts being the guarantee of what he has in store for us (Romans 8:23).

Prophets

The line of prophets stretched from Moses to John the Baptist, and was continued (in the New Testament) though in rather a different form.

We notice that they were men called by God (Isaiah 6. Jeremiah 1:4-19). It was not a career which a man chose for himself, but a call from God to which, sometimes with reluctance (Exodus 3:11), he responded. There was always this feature of a direct commission from God. The prophets came from his side to stand before men (1 Kings 17:1). In the second place they were men with a message. It was the sign of a true prophet that he never proclaimed his own ideas, but only what God had told him to say. Exactly how the message came to him differed. Very often we are simply told that 'the word of the Lord came ...' (Hosea 1:1 &c), or that in some way God put his words into the mouth of his servant (Exodus 4:15), perhaps by means of a vision or a dream (Numbers 12:6).

96

The kind of message also differed. Sometimes it was a personal message that God wanted to convey to one man, as for example the message that Nathan took to David (2 Samuel 7:4,5). Sometimes it was more in the nature of a sermon on the moral and social condition of the country, and many of the Minor Prophets' proclamations were of this sort (e.g. Hosea. Amos). Sometimes too they were required to reveal things which were not yet known. These might concern the present (2 Kings 6:12) or the future; near (2 Samuel 12:10-12) or distant events (Isaiah 9 and 53). It is perhaps in connexion with this particular side to their ministry that they were sometimes called 'Seers' (1 Samuel 9:9). We notice too that while many of them ploughed a lonely furrow, some enjoyed a definite status, and the Kings of Israel seem to have looked upon them as a kind of moral and spiritual adviser—a sort of court chaplain—to whom they could turn for counsel and advice, even though, as was often the case, they refused to take it. Thus we find Nathan in close touch with David (2 Samuel 12:1), Isaiah with Hezekiah (2 Kings 20:1), and Elisha with Jehoshaphat (2 Kings 3:11). They may have undergone some sort of training (2 Kings 6:1,2), and the great respect in which they were held in the country is seen in the phrase which is often applied to them, 'the man of God' (2 Kings 5:8).

When we turn to the New Testament we find that the prophetic ministry is still continued. The predictive element is not quite so prominent as in the Old Testament, though we still have instances of it in the warnings of Agabus (Acts 11:28; 21:10,11), and of course in written form in the Book of Revelation; but there is a sense in which all Christians are called upon to prophesy and proclaim the message of Jesus Christ, and warn people of the consequences of rejecting it. There also appears to be a special gift of prophecy with which some Christians were endowed (1 Corinthians 14:22-25, 29-32) and others were not. Exactly what this gift was we cannot be sure, but it seems clear that prophets did not discover new sources of truth to the Church, but rather expounded truth already revealed; and perhaps in this sense the gift is still exercised today by those with a special insight into the meaning of God's word, and an aptitude for explaining the faith as it has been revealed to us in the Bible.

It is important to notice the warnings against 'false prophets' which frequently occur in the Bible (Matthew 24:11. 1 John 4:1). There does not appear to be any single test of authenticity, but the

97

Bible lays down certain principles. If what a man predicted did not come to pass, then this in itself was a ground for suspicion (Deuteronomy 18:22). If what he taught was in any way contradicted by what God had already revealed of his will, then he must be rejected (Deuteronomy 13:1-5. 1 John 4:1,2). If the prophet himself is living an unworthy and immoral life, then his teaching is invalidated (Jeremiah 23:10-14), and he must not be listened to.

Propitiation

The word only appears twice in the AV (Romans 3:25 and 1 John 2:2), and in both cases it has been abandoned in the RSV and NEB in favour of the word 'expiation', no doubt because the word 'propitiation' suggested the pacifying of an angry and capricious God.

The distinction between the two words is an important one. In simple terms, to 'expiate' means to 'put things right' and to 'propitiate' means to 'appease'. If I damage my neighbour's garden wall, I may put it right at my own expense, but I have not necessarily regained his favour. I have expiated my offence, but I have not conciliated the person. 'Propitiation' always has this personal dimension.

That Christ's death mended the damage caused by man's sin is an important truth; but the Bible also makes it clear that it turned away God's wrath (Romans 1:18), not by changing his mind towards us, but by fulfilling his purpose of loving justice for mankind. The 'wrath of God' (Ephesians 5:6) towards sinful man is an aspect of his character which runs right through the Bible (Psalm 7:11), and it is this which makes propitiation necessary if we are once again to enjoy his favour and fellowship.

It is important to note finally that Christ is not spoken of as the 'propitiator', but the 'propitiation'. He is the offering as well as the priest. A propitiator might make use of means of propitiation outside himself, but Christ is our propitiation, just as in another place he is said to be our 'redemption' (1 Corinthians 1:30).

98

Reconciliation
(See also GOSPEL)
This word implies that enmity has been removed, and friendly
relations re-established between two people. It is the word used in
the New Testament to describe the fact that by dying to remove
man's sin, Jesus also removed the barrier between man and God,
thus making friendship possible (Romans 5:10. Colossians 1:21). It
is noteworthy that the New Testament always speaks of man and
not God being reconciled; God is propitiated (see article), but man
is reconciled. This message of reconciliation, the news that a peace
treaty has been brought about through the mediation of Jesus
Christ, has now been committed to Christians to pass on to others
(2 Corinthians 5:18-20).

Redemption
A ransom in Bible days was the price paid to set free a slave or a
prisoner, and even in some cases a man who had committed a crime
(Exodus 21:28-30); while it was also the term used for certain legal
transactions between kinsmen (Ruth 4). The person who paid the
ransom was known as the 'Redeemer', and his act as one of
'Redemption'. It was a popular metaphor in the Old Testament,
and God is spoken of as a Redeemer (Isaiah 43:1,3), and is described

99

as redeeming his people from Egypt (2 Samuel 7:23) and Babylon (Jeremiah 15:21), and from national (Psalm 25:22) and personal (Psalm 26:11) trouble.

Quite naturally therefore this familiar idea was carried over into the New Testament, for man was the slave and prisoner of sin (John 8:34. Romans 6:17), and the sacrifice of Christ upon the cross was the ransom price paid to set him free (Mark 10:45. 1 Peter 1:18,19). This redemption sprang from the grace of God (Romans 3:24), it was procured by the blood of Christ (Ephesians 1:7), it is enjoyed through the faith of the individual, and it results in a life lived under an entirely new ownership (1 Corinthians 6:19,20).

Regeneration

The idea of national (Ezekiel 36:25-27) and personal (Isaiah 57:15) renewal is present in the Old Testament, but assumes greater prominence in the New Testament, although the word 'regeneration' itself only appears twice (Matthew 19:28 AV. Titus 3:5 AV, RSV).

It is in John's Gospel that the beginning of this new life is described for us. We are to be 'born again' in a spiritual sense, through the initiative of God and the operation of the Holy Spirit (John 3:3-8), and this new birth qualifies us for God's Kingdom, and brings us into a new relationship with him as members of his family (John 1:12).

Paul carries the teaching on this subject further, showing us that in Christ we are 'a new creation' (2 Corinthians 5:17), not just morally reformed, but regenerated. This 'new man' (Ephesians 4:24) with new tastes and ambitions begins to walk 'in newness of life' (Romans 6:4).

Finally, in John's first epistle we find this 'newness of life' spelt out in rather more detail. It means a new intellectual outlook, for we believe that Jesus Christ is God (1 John 5:1); a new moral outlook upon sin and righteousness (1 John 2:29; 3:9); a new social outlook towards others (1 John 4:7); and a new practical outlook when faced with the sinful pressures of the world (1 John 5:4,18).

Religion

In its popular, everyday use this word describes one of the great recognized systems of faith and worship, such as Christianity, Islam and Buddhism, and it is difficult to see at first sight why the NEB should have chosen it to translate the Greek word *eusebeia* which is almost always rendered 'godliness' in the AV and RSV (1

Timothy 2:2,10; 3:16; 4:7 &c). Perhaps the most accurate translation would be 'piety in action' (James 1:26,27), and it may have been felt that the average reader would tend to describe such a person as 'religious', and for this reason the word was used.

Repentance

Repentance in the New Testament sense is a God-given change of heart (Romans 2:4. 2 Timothy 2:25) towards sin, righteousness and God himself—an idea which of course was already present in the Old Testament even if expressed in different words (2 Kings 17:13 &c).

Repentance is the first and most important condition for the forgiveness of sins (Luke 24:47. Acts 2:38; 3:19), because God cannot forgive what we are not prepared to forsake (Isaiah 55:7). It is often accompanied by genuine and heartfelt sorrow (Luke 22:62. 2 Corinthians 7:9), always results in a new way of life (Matthew 3:8. Acts 26:20), and is the cause of great joy in the presence of God (Luke 15:7).

When we read in the Old Testament of God repenting (e.g. Jonah 3:10) it means not that he changed his mind but that man's repentance had enabled God to reveal a different side of his character.

Resurrection

The resurrection is represented for us in the Bible in three ways.
1. *A past fact.* It was an historical event which took place when Jesus, having been put to death, rose again from the grave. This event he had foretold during his earthly life (Mark 9:9. John 16:16), and there were even passages in the Old Testament which were later seen to apply to it (Acts 2:27. Psalm 16:10).

It is made quite clear that the resurrection of Jesus was altogether different from the revival of Lazarus (John 11:44) and others whom Jesus raised. In their case there was simply a return from death, but he passed right through it into another dimension of life. He was the same, and yet different. Although his disciples knew him, they did not always recognize him at once (Luke 24:31,36,37. John 20:15). He could be seen (Matthew 28:9) and heard and touched (Luke 24:39. John 20:17), and yet he could come and go mysteriously, passing through closed doors as if they were not there (Luke 24:31. John 20:19).

The disciples made little attempt to prove the fact of the resurrection, for the simple reason that they felt the onus of proof to be on the other side, the unbelievers. If Jesus did not rise, then either his friends stole the body—escaping detection, deceiving the authorities, spreading a lie, and, in the case of some of them, accepting martyrdom for what was a gigantic hoax; or his enemies did it, in which case we must ask why they were so agitated when they heard that the body was missing, making up a story to account for its disappearance (Matthew 28:11-15), and why they never produced it to demolish the myth of a resurrection when it began to spread. The third possibility, that Jesus never actually died, but swooned, and revived in the tomb sufficiently to make his escape and rally his disciples, need not be taken seriously. Apart from the endless difficulties it raises, it contradicts the official recognition of the fact that he was dead (Mark 15:44,45).

2. *A present experience.* Because Jesus rose from the dead, he is alive for evermore (Revelation 1:18), and Christians may enjoy his presence, through the Person of his Holy Spirit (John 16:7) as genuinely as if he were actually amongst them himself.

Further, the Christian is someone who is spiritually identified with the death and resurrection of Jesus. It is as though he himself had died upon the cross and then been raised into newness of life (Romans 6:4-11). He is 'risen with Christ' (Colossians 3:1) to a new life of holiness and victory over sin. Just as the death of Christ broke the guilt of sin, so his resurrection can break its power, and the Christian is called to share in and enjoy that triumphant experience.

3. *A future hope.* It follows that because Jesus rose from the dead, and opened the gate to immortality (2 Timothy 1:10), those who believe in him will also one day share this resurrection life. Just as death was brought into the world by one man, so the conquest of death has been brought into the world by Jesus Christ (1 Corinthians 15:20-23). We have been given this living hope (1 Peter 1:3) of a resurrection when we shall be equipped with a new spiritual body (1 Corinthians 15:46), perfectly adapted to an entirely new kind of existence, when we shall

'Learn all we lacked before; hear, know, and say
What this tumultuous body now denies;
And feel, who have laid our groping hand away;
And see, no longer blinded by our eyes.'

Revelation

The Bible assumes throughout that if God is to be known, it can only be in so far as he chooses to reveal himself. His answer to the question in the book of Job, 'Can you by searching find out the deep things of God?' (Job 11:7) is an emphatic 'No'. Sinful, blinded human nature cannot uncover the mysteries of a transcendent God. The initiative must lie with God himself. In fact he has chosen to reveal himself to man in three ways.

1. *In Nature.* Paul tells his readers that they have no excuse for their ignorance of God, because the visible creation clearly reveals 'his eternal power and deity' (Romans 1:20); and the psalmist is making the same point when he says, 'The heavens declare the glory of God; and the firmament showeth his handywork' (Psalm 19:1). Looked at by thoughtful, reverent eyes, these things at the very least speak of a Creator who knew the meaning of beauty, power and order.

2. *In the Bible.* The first and most important aspect of God's revelation of himself was that he was *personal.* Man realized from the start that he was not dealing with some impersonal, cosmic force, but with someone with whom he could communicate, however far beyond his own limited understanding he might stretch (Genesis 2:15-17). This truth was never lost sight of; and as God's people came to realize that this Person was their Creator, King, Judge and Father, it was this that distinguished the God of Israel from all others.

Next they learned that God was a *moral* being. That is to say, he was concerned with behaviour. His first word to man was a command (Genesis 2:16), with a penalty attached for disobedience; and it quickly became very apparent to people that the Lord their God was holy (Leviticus 19:2).

Finally, as time went on, they came to see that God was *spiritual.* Although they could worship him in their temple, he was not confined to human buildings or to any one place. He inhabits eternity, and at the same time lives with those of a humble and contrite spirit (Isaiah 57:15). He was with his people in their own country, and with Daniel and his friends in Babylon during the exile (Daniel 6:10). Nowhere in heaven or earth can be called 'God-forsaken' (Psalm 139:7-12), and we cannot escape from his presence any more than we can escape from the wind.

3. *In Jesus Christ.* It is here that the revelation of God's person and will are perfected. 'He who has seen me,' said Jesus, 'has seen the Father' (John 14:9). It was as people watched him and heard him that they saw the splendour of God—his holiness, power and love.

103

Just as light can only be appreciated properly in the form of a rainbow, so Jesus revealed the true qualities of God, who is the unapproachable light (1 Timothy 6:16).

No one has ever seen God, but Jesus Christ has embodied him for us (John 1:18. Colossians 2:9); and it is only in him that we see 'the reflection of God's glory, and the very stamp of his nature' (Hebrews 1:2,3. 2 Corinthians 4:6). And this picture, presented to us in the Gospels, is more fully amplified and explained in the later books of the New Testament (John 16:12,13).

There is of course a limit to what can be revealed by the Holy Spirit here and now to even the most receptive and spiritually-minded men and women. Indeed, the more we know of God, the more we find we don't know. As Paul says, 'How unsearchable are his judgements, and his ways past finding out! For who has known the mind of the Lord? or who has been his counsellor?' (Romans 11:33,34). There are divine depths which we shall never be able to fathom in this life, and for which we shall need eternity to complete the revelation. 'Now we see only puzzling reflections in a mirror, but then we shall see face to face. My knowledge now is partial; then it will be whole, like God's knowledge of me' (1 Corinthians 13:12,13 NEB).

Righteousness

1. *Divine righteousness.* Running right through the Old Testament is the theme of God's righteousness, that is to say, the absolute justice and fairness of his dealings with his creatures. 'The Lord is righteous in all his ways' (Psalm 145:17), we are told; and in one place he is called, 'The Lord is our Righteousness' (Jeremiah 23:6). As he deals with us, so he wants to see us deal with our fellow men and women (Micah 6:8), and the teaching of the Old Testament on this subject could be summed up in the words of Psalm 11:7—'The righteous Lord loves righteous deeds'.

2. *Legal righteousness.* But however great his moral effort may be, man can never produce a righteousness which measures up to God's requirements or undo the effects of his sin. Judged by God's standards, man's righteousness is like 'a polluted garment' (Isaiah 64:6). Paul realized the futility of this exercise, and that if he was to be accepted by God it could never be on the grounds of his own righteousness (Romans 10:1-6. Philippians 3:9. Titus 3:5).

3. *Imputed righteousness.* The only way in which we can stand before God is if we are clothed in the righteousness which he alone

104

can provide as a free gift to be received by faith. (See Romans 3:22 where 'the righteousness of God' might be compared to 'the tailor's coat'—the one he provides for his customers, not the one he wears himself). It is given to all who make Christ their Saviour (Romans 4:6. 1 Corinthians 1:30. 2 Corinthians 5:21). It is like the 'wedding garment' provided by a nobleman for his guests to cover up their deficiencies and also reflect his own splendour (Matthew 22:11,12. Isaiah 61:10).

4. *Spiritual righteousness.* One of the fruits of the new life is 'righteousness' (Philippians 1:11)—just, fair, generous, kind behaviour; and in the life of every Christian this should begin to appear quite naturally as a result of the Holy Spirit's presence in his heart (Ephesians 4:24).

Sabbath

The word comes from the root *sabbat,* meaning to 'cease' or 'desist', and we find it in Genesis 2:3 (NEB) where we read that 'God ceased from all his work' on the seventh day. This divine example became the basis of the Fourth Commandment (Exodus 20:8-11) which forbade work of any kind on the Sabbath; and it is interesting to see how this commandment worked out in practice in such matters as farming (Exodus 34:21), household duties (Exodus 35:1-3), the demands made upon others (Exodus 20:10) and the collecting of the manna (Exodus 16:22-30).

But the Sabbath was more than a day of rest, and is spoken of as belonging to the Lord. Reference is made to 'my Sabbaths' (Isaiah 56:4-6) and 'my holy day' (Isaiah 58:13) on which God's will and pleasure were to be sought, and not man's. As such, the Jewish Sabbath became a sacrament of the people's relationship to him, and a sign for other nations to see of the covenant which existed between them and their God (Exodus 31:13-17); and this fact was strongly emphasised during the period of restoration under Nehemiah, when he found the commandment being abused by those who remained behind during the exile (Nehemiah 10:31; 13:15-22).

But as in all sacraments, there is a danger of the symbol becoming the whole, and the shadow being valued more than the substance,

106

and this is what happened in the period between the Old and New Testaments. The regulations regarding the Sabbath became so strict that pious Jews allowed themselves to be killed in battle rather than defend their lives on that day; and it was during this time also that there were added the petty and ritualistic rules which were so roundly condemned by Jesus. In attacking these accretions, he was not attacking the commandment itself; but while he was careful to observe the Sabbath (Luke 4:16), he insisted that acts of necessity (such as getting food) and acts of mercy must be allowed to continue (Matthew 12:1-13).

After the resurrection, which occurred on the first day of the week, Christians began to use that day rather than the seventh for worship, fellowship and Christian service (Acts 20:7. 1 Corinthians 16:2), though it is probable that many of them also continued to observe the Jewish Sabbath (Colossians 2:16), a matter on which Paul pleaded for tolerance and liberty of conscience (Romans 14:5). But it is important to note that in the instructions sent by the Church Leaders to Gentile Christians no mention is made about Sabbath observance (Acts 15), and this may have been because its intention and purpose had been fulfilled in the coming of Christ. In other words (as Augustine argued), the shadow had given way to the reality, and Christ provided the perfect, spiritual rest for ll to enjoy who would come to him (Matthew 11:28. Hebrews 4:9).

As Christianity spread into the Gentile world, therefore, the Sabbath as such was abandoned, but the difficult question remains as to how far, if at all, the prohibitions attached to it have been transferred and now apply to the Christian Sunday. Luther insisted that Sunday was an entirely new Christian institution without any Jewish foundation; whereas the opposite view was taken by the English Puritans, who argued that the day should be observed as a 'Christian Sabbath'.

There is room for discussion here, and even tolerant disagreement, but it is perhaps more profitable to stress the positive side, and to say that Christians of all countries and of every tradition have seen in Sunday a special God-given opportunity for Christian activity, worship and fellowship, and consequently a rest from things that engage their time, energy and attention for the remainder of the week.

Sacrifice

Very early in the Old Testament we read of sacrifices, such as those made by Cain and Abel (Genesis 4:1-5) and Noah (Genesis 8:20-22), and though the original idea seems to have been that of thanksgiving, the thought of expiating sins that they had committed was likely also to have been present; while sacrifices too played an important part in the making of covenants (Genesis 15; Exodus 24:8).

Perhaps the next important stage was the sacrifice of the Passover (Exodus 12) which was ever afterwards celebrated as a family festival in memory of the escape from Egypt. It was seen as a prophecy and a picture of the death of Jesus which brought deliverance from sin (1 Corinthians 5:7), and there are several points of close identity. The lamb had to be 'without blemish' (1 Peter 1:18,19), then it had to be slain, and finally the blood had to be applied to the door posts, signifying personal faith on the part of the house-holder in the sacrifice that had been made. The development of the sacrificial system in the Old Testament is perhaps most fully explained in Leviticus 1-7, where we read about the different kinds of sacrifice required and the precise ritual surrounding them. They vary considerably in detail, but many of them had five things in common. The person making the sacrifice identified himself with the victim by putting his hand on its head (Leviticus 1:4); the animal was slain (Leviticus 1:5); its blood was sprinkled (Leviticus 1:5), symbolizing the actual atonement; much of the carcase was burnt (Leviticus 1:7-10), to show that it was acceptable to God; and sometimes part of it was eaten (Leviticus 6:16) as a sign of fellowship based on the sacrifice that had been made.

It is chiefly in the Book of Hebrews that the Old Testament sacrifices are applied symbolically to the death of Christ, and the purpose seems to be to show that in at least two respects his sacrifice was immeasurably superior to those which foreshadowed it. First, it was *perfect* in a way no animal sacrifice could be, because Jesus was without sin (Hebrews 9:11-18); and secondly, because he was the Son of God, it was a once-for-all, *eternal* sacrifice (Hebrews 7:27; 10:1-13) which need never, like the Old Testament sacrifices, be repeated.

The word 'sacrifice' is also applied to Christians, for in return for what Christ has done for them, they are to present themselves to him as 'a living sacrifice' (Romans 12:1). What this means in practice, we can see from other parts of the New Testament. For some it meant the offering of money or other material gifts to those in special need (Romans 15:16,17. Philippians 4:18); for others it meant Christian service of some sort or another which was acceptable to God (Hebrews 13:15,16); while for Paul it involved inprisonment (Philippians 2:17) and eventually martyrdom (2 Timothy 4:6).

Salvation

In the Old Testament the word usually had a physical or material meaning, and was applied to those occasions when God brought deliverance to his people from their enemies, or from illness or disaster (Exodus 14:13) but as time went on, it began to assume a more moral or spiritual meaning (Isaiah 12:3), and by the time we get to the New Testament it was almost exclusively used in this sense.

It is in fact another 'portmanteau' word which includes all the aspects of our deliverance from the guilt and power of sin—redemption, reconciliation, cleansing and justification. While its roots lie deep in the Old Testament (2 Timothy 3:15. Isaiah 53 &c), its full fruit appears with the coming of the gospel—the complete revelation of God's saving power (Romans 1:16). It originates in the grace of God (Titus 2:11) and the death of Christ; and it is received by faith (Ephesians 2:8-10), and is worked out in the life of the Christian in consecration to God (Philippians 2:12).

There are in fact three phases or tenses of salvation. The believer has been saved from the penalty of sin (Ephesians 2:8), he is being saved day by day from its power (1 Corinthians 1:18), and he will one day be saved from its presence, becoming immune to the attacks of temptation, when he goes to be with Christ (Romans 13:11. 1 Thessalonians 5:9. 1 Peter 1:5). In this respect the Christian is like someone who has inherited a fortune. Part of it is an outright gift, which he can possess and enjoy at once and use to pay his outstanding debts. Part of it is in the form of a steady income which has been designed to last a lifetime. Part is held in trust until he marries, perhaps, or reaches a certain age.

Saint

Nowadays the word 'saint' is used either as an honorific title e.g. St. Augustine, St. Joan), or to describe someone who exhibits unusual Christian qualities, and of whom we say, 'He is an absolute saint'. But this is not the original meaning of the word. It comes from the same root as the word 'sanctification' (see article), and means someone who is set apart for God to be owned and used by him. As such it is one of the most popular words in the New Testament for describing ordinary Christians — although in the modern translations it is often translated simply as God's holy people or God's people (e.g. 1 Corinthians 1:2); and though the New Testament makes the charitable assumption that they were 'saintly' in character as well as 'saintly' in name, we have only to read other parts of 1 Corinthians to see that they did not always live up to that meaning of the word. It is possible to be a Christian without being Christ-like, but the Christian's ideal should always be to follow Christ.

Sanctification (Sanctify)
The word means 'dedication' or 'consecration', and in the Old Testament was applied to any person or object 'set apart' for the service of God. The NEB generally prefers the word 'Holy' or 'Hallowed'. The Sabbath Day, for example, was 'hallowed' (Genesis 2:3), and so were the priests (Exodus 28:41); while God himself is spoken of sometimes as being 'sanctified' (Isaiah 8:13) in the sense that he is totally separated from man's sin, and lives in unapproachable light (1 Timothy 6:16).
In the New Testament the word is applied almost exclusively to the spiritual condition of the Christian. There is a sense in which he is 'sanctified' already (1 Peter 1:2), but another sense in which sanctification is a life-long process (1 Thessalonians 4:3). A man who becomes a naturalised Englishman is officially and technically English from that moment on, but the 'anglicizing' process will go on for many years, and only gradually will he become English in habit and outlook. So it may be correct to speak of a Christian as a 'saint' (see article), but that does not mean that all at once he is 'saintly' or 'sanctified'.

Satan
The word means 'adversary', and in the Old Testament we find Satan opposing God's servants like Job (Job 1:6-12) and David (1 Chronicles 21:1), while it is clearly he who is working through the 'serpent' in the garden of Eden (Genesis 3:1).
When we turn to the New Testament his presence becomes even more apparent. From the very start of Jesus' ministry Satan opposed him (Matthew 4:1-11), trying to undermine the work which he came to do (Mark 4:15. Matthew 13:38,39). He demanded to have Simon Peter (Luke 22:31,32 AV), 'entered into' Judas

Iscariot (Luke 22:3) and filled the heart of Ananias (Acts 5:3). He could use different disguises, appearing sometimes as a roaring lion, in overwhelming strength (1 Peter 5:8), sometimes as an angel of light, with all the subtlety of a serpent (2 Corinthians 11:14), sometimes even in the person of a friend (Matthew 16:23); and it seems too that just as God is served by angels (see article), so there are diabolical agents carrying out the purposes of Satan. The Christian must not be ignorant of his devices (2 Corinthians 2:11) but realize that stripped of his disguises, he is a deceiver (Revelation 12:9), a liar and a murderer (John 8:44). Nor are we to be afraid of him, for equipped with the whole armour of God (Ephesians 6:11) and 'firm in faith' (1 Peter 5:9), we may resist all his onslaughts.

The Bible has little to say about the origin of Satan, though there may well be allusions to this in Isaiah 14:12-14. At times his power looks absolute. Indeed, he is called 'The ruler of this world' (John 14:30), and we are told that 'the whole godless world lies in the power of the evil one' (1 John 5:19 NEB); and in what are called 'the last days' we must even be prepared for him to set up some kind of counterfeit Messiah (2 Thessalonians 2:3-10). But his power is strictly limited. It was to destroy him that Jesus came into the world (1 John 3:8), and the Bible leaves us in no doubt at all about his final defeat (Romans 16:20) and overthrow (Matthew 25:41. Revelation 20:10).

Saviour

In the Old Testament the word 'Saviour' was usually applied to God in his capacity as Deliverer of the nation from disaster. For instance, he was referred to as 'The hope of Israel, their Saviour in time of trouble' (Jeremiah 14:8 NEB). But like the word 'salvation' (see article), the word came to assume a more spiritual significance. When we turn to the New Testament therefore, we find that the name 'Jesus' was chosen because it meant 'Saviour' or 'Deliverer' (Matthew 1:21—the New Testament equivalent to 'Joshua') and signified the work which he had come into the world to do. It was as a 'Saviour' that the most spiritually-minded and percipient greeted him (Luke 1:47; 2:11,30), for they realized that though he had also come to reveal God to man, his first and most important task was to reconcile man to God by dying for us upon the cross and bearing the guilt of our sin; and that 'the Father sent the Son to be the Saviour of the world' (1 John 4:14 AV, NEB).

111

Scriptures

(See also INSPIRATION)

This is the word by which, in New Testament days, the Old Testament writings were known, and the many allusions to 'the Scriptures' refer to some part of the Law, the Prophets or the other writings.

It is clear from the very reverent way in which they were spoken of, that they were not regarded as ordinary human writings, but as 'breathed out by God' into the minds of the writers (2 Timothy 3:16. 2 Peter 1:20,21); Jesus himself stamped them with his own authority when he said they could not be broken (John 10.35), and by using them on many occasions to prove and explain the work he had come to do (Luke 24:27). Although the structure of the Old Testament was not officially recognized until towards the end of the first century AD, its authority was accepted by the Palestinian Jews by the time of Jesus in practically the same form as we have it today.

After the resurrection, the words of Jesus himself were accepted as authoritative (1 Corinthians 7:10,12), and put on a level with the Old Testament; while before long Paul s writings too were recognized to have an authority which put them alongside 'the other Scriptures' (2 Peter 3:15,16). This was not to be wondered at when we remember the promise of Jesus that his Holy Spirit would lead his disciples into truths which they were not at that time ready to learn (John 16:12,13). In several places the Christian is encouraged to study the Scriptures, and we find some people called 'the Bereans' commended for making this a daily practice (Acts 17:11). The reason for doing so is that the Scriptures bear witness to Christ, foreshadowing many of the events of his life (John 5:39); they 'lead us to salvation through faith in Christ Jesus' (2 Timothy 3:15 NEB); they help us to build our lives on sound moral and spiritual principles (2 Timothy 3:16,17); and they enable us to become powerful in our use of them when trying to help others also (Acts 18:24-28).

Servant

The word 'servant' is used in our English versions to translate two different Greek words, *diakanos* (minister or deacon (see article)), and *doulos* which means slave. This is the more usual, and it is the word Paul often applies to himself at the start of his letters (Romans 1:1. Philippians 1:1).

112

The two principal ways in which a man or woman became a slave were by capture (usually as a result of war) or purchase; and it is in these two ways that the Christian is regarded in the New Testament as belonging to Christ.

First, he has been 'captured' from sin and Satan (Romans 6:16,17) and passed into the possession of a new master. 'Christ once took hold of me', or 'arrested' me, wrote Paul (Philippians 3:12 NEB), as he looked back to the time of his capture on the Damascus Road. Secondly, the Christian has been redeemed (1 Peter 1:18,19) or 'bought at a price' (1 Corinthians 6:20 NEB). He has become the property of a new owner, and all that he has—time, talents, money and property—pass into the possession of that person.

It is important to note that it was as a Servant that Jesus saw his ministry (Mark 10:45. Luke 22:27), thus fulfilling the prophetic picture of the Messiah as portrayed in the Old Testament (Isaiah 42:1-4; 52:13-53:12), and at the same time providing a pattern and a motive for the life of service expected of his followers (John 13:13,14).

Sin

This is the word used throughout the Bible to describe wrong-doing in relation to God, and though it expresses itself in many forms, the underlying factor is always this idea of a disobedient, ungrateful, rebellious attitude towards a holy and righteous God (Psalm 51:4).

There are several words used to describe this state of affairs, each with its own particular emphasis. Thus 'sin' itself means to 'fall short' (Romans 3:23), and was the word used of a spear which had missed its target. It is a failure to reach the standards set by God, notably in the Ten Commandments.

'Iniquity' on the other hand means 'unequal' or 'out of line'. It suggests something that is twisted, a deviation from the set path. It is the failure to follow the course which God has provided, and is like an attempt to copy a straight line without the aid of a ruler (Isaiah 53:6).

'Transgression' or 'Lawlessness' (1 John 3:4) is the breaking of God's law, and introduces a legal aspect into sin; for in all forms of society there are penalties attached to the deliberate breaking of a law.

'Trespass' (Ephesians 2:1 AV) really means a false step, and suggests someone getting out of bounds or missing the way; and it

113

is interesting to notice in this connexion that the three main words for 'sin' in the Old Testament are variations on the idea of losing one's way, leaving the path, or refusing to get on to the right way. 'Trespass' has a more personal application than some of the other words, and is used to describe the way we offend against each other (Matthew 6:14,15).

'Unrighteousness' describes the state of the human heart (Romans 3:10-18). It pictures the disease from which the heart of man is suffering (Jeremiah 17:9), the polluted river from which flow as a matter of course pride, envy, hatred, malice and so on (Mark 7:21-23).

It is clear from what we read in the Bible that sin entered the world from outside, for in the first instance everything that God created was 'very good' (Genesis 1:31). We must assume therefore that in some pre-cosmic existence Satan rebelled against God (perhaps in the manner described in Isaiah 14:12-15), and thereby became the origin of evil in every form. From the moment of man's disobedience, it passed into the world, in that way infecting the whole human race ever since (Psalm 51:5. Romans 5:12).

The results of sin are set out plainly in the Bible. The harmony which should have existed between men has been fatally disrupted (James 4:1). The whole creation has been dislocated, and is awaiting its own final redemption (Romans 8:19-22); while for the individual himself it has brought defilement (Mark 7:21-23), slavery (John 8:34) and death (see article) (Romans 6:23).

It was man's sin that brought Christ into the world, that he might undo its consequences. He bore its penalty (2 Corinthians 5:21), cleansed its stain (1 John 1:7) and broke its power (Hebrews 2:14,15). He made possible once again freedom of access into God's presence (Ephesians 2:18. 1 Peter 3:18), peace between men (Galatians 3:28. Ephesians 2:15) and victory over temptation (Romans 6:14).

Finally, the Bible leaves us with a picture of things as they will be when Satan's power is eventually destroyed. It began with a picture of a garden, from which the sinner was expelled (Genesis 3:24); and it ends with one of a city from which sin itself, in every shape or form, will be excluded, where nothing that is unclean shall enter (Revelation 21:27), and where God himself will reign in a society in which harmony and peace have taken the place of discord and strife (Isaiah 11).

T

Temptation

Until the 17th Century, the English word 'temptation' had a neutral flavour, and could be used to describe any test, whether the purpose was good or evil. Thus in the AV we read that 'God did tempt Abraham' (Genesis 22:1) in the matter of sacrificing Isaac, meaning that he put him to the test; and the Greek word translated 'tempt' in the New Testament is also translated 'prove' (John 6:6 AV) and 'examine' (2 Corinthians 13:5), on both occasions in a favourable sense. Again, the NEB translation of 'Lead us not into temptation' is more correctly rendered, 'Do not bring us to the test' (Matthew 6:13), because God cannot entice people to do evil (James 1:13).

Therefore although the word has developed this more sinister meaning, and is now always used in connexion with some form of inducement to do evil, it still contains the idea of testing or proving, because although perpetrated by Satan, it is allowed by God for our good, and that is why Christians are actually told to rejoice in it (James 1:2) as well as endure it (James 1:12).

Sometimes the confrontation will be direct and personal, as it was between Eve and the serpent (Genesis 3) and between Jesus and the Devil (Matthew 4:1-11). At other times the temptation will come

115

through a third person. It was in that way that Adam fell, and again Jesus recognized the voice of Satan in the suggestion of one of his closest friends (Matthew 16:22,23). While on other occasions the temptation comes from within, from our own baser desires (James 1:13-15). Sometimes we are tempted by the Devil himself, sometimes by the world, and sometimes by the flesh.

It is important to remember that temptation is not sin, or else Jesus himself would not have been tempted (Hebrews 4:15); but giving way to it is sin; that the temptation itself can actually be beneficial, strengthening and preparing us for great responsibilities (1 Peter 1:6,7); and that God will never allow it to become stronger than we can bear, but will always provide a way of escape (1 Corinthians 10:13) for those who will watch and pray (Matthew 26:41).

Testament
(See COVENANT)

Tongues
There are two places where the phenomenon of speaking in tongues is mentioned, Acts (notably in Chapter 2) and 1 Corinthians 12 and 14.

1. A remarkable feature of Pentecost was the way in which the apostles were able to speak so that those who listened to them heard about the wonderful works of God in their own native tongues (Acts 2:4-11). The use of the Greek word *dialektos* makes it clear that they were speaking in perfectly intelligible languages, but ones which they had never learnt. Symbolically this event reversed the curse of Babel (Genesis 11:1-9), proving that the gospel had a universal message which was intended for all the nations of the world.

2. When we turn to 1 Corinthians, we must ask ourselves whether we find the same phenomenon or something quite different. Was the gift described there the ability to speak in a foreign language which the speaker had never learnt, or was it, as the NEB suggests, some form of ecstatic utterance?

Those who hold to the latter view argue that at Corinth the gift had to be sought, while at Pentecost it was freely bestowed; that an interpreter was required at Corinth, but not at Pentecost; that the word *dialektos* (language) is never found in the Corinthian passages (and that when Paul refers to languages in 1 Corinthians 14:10 he uses a different word); that the word *glossa* (tongue) had

116

come to be used in classical Greek for bold, poetic terms such as belonged to epic poetry (Aristotle Rhet, iii. 3,10); and that because the gift can be counterfeited in other religions it is not thereby invalidated, any more than the miracles of Jesus were invalidated by false wonder-workers. All this, they maintain, justifies the use of the phrase 'ecstatic utterance', and, though it does not necessarily exclude genuine languages, it does include a form of speech not known to men which, as it were, 'takes over' when the worshipper can no longer express himself in ordinary human language.

Those on the other hand who maintain that the two manifestations are the same point to the obvious similarities. They argue that the normal use of the word *glossa*, whatever exceptions there may have been, was 'language'; that Paul insisted on an interpreter at Corinth because (unlike Pentecost) only one speaker at a time was permitted; that God would not endow his people with a gift which enabled them to speak in meaningless gibberish; and that modern psychology can find an explanation for certain forms of ecstatic utterance, but rarely for speaking in an intelligible but unlearnt language.

There may be no final and conclusive answer to this question, and, without allowing it to divide them, Christians may have to agree to differ. But there are two important things which must be said in conclusion. First, there are those who think that unless a Christian possesses this particular gift he is in some way spiritually deficient. This view can find absolutely no support in the New Testament, and indeed Paul himself completely demolishes it by asking the question, 'Do all speak with tongues?' (1 Corinthians 12:30).

Secondly, the gift has certain dangers which Paul (who possessed it to a remarkable degree—1 Corinthians 14:18) recognized at once. It seems that the Christians at Corinth were attaching an exaggerated importance to the gift, and seeking it rather than the others, perhaps because it was one of the more obvious and spectacular, or perhaps simply because they wanted to show off. Such an attitude could lead only to pride and divisiveness, and so Paul tried to put the whole thing in perspective, regulating its use with certain strict rules, and relegating the gift itself to a far less important position. At the same time he urged his readers to pursue the best gifts (1 Corinthians 12:31) of which, he regarded prophecy (see article) to be the greatest, because it could not fail to edify the hearers, whereas speaking in tongues, unless there was the corresponding gift of interpretation, merely left them confused.

117

Transgression
(See SIN)

Trespass
(See SIN)

Trinity

This word, like some others we are considering, is not actually found in the Bible, but was introduced into the Christian vocabulary to describe a phenomenon which is revealed there. It means 'tri-unity' or 'three-in-one', and is the word applied to God who seems to reveal himself to us in three distinct and yet inseparable ways.

At the time of Jesus, the Jews were of course monotheistic, that is to say, they believed only in one God, and not polytheistic, like many of the surrounding tribes and nations. The doctrine of the Trinity developed out of the disciples' encounter with God which took more than one form. Taught to believe in one God, it became perfectly clear to them that Jesus claimed to be equal with God (John 10:30-38; 14:10,11; 17:21), and that the Holy Spirit, whom he promised to send (John 14:17,18) and whom they later received on the Day of Pentecost (Acts 2:1-4), must also be thought of as God. It was as though the same God was looking at them through three different windows at once—nature, history and experience. This is why the New Testament, and especially the epistles, is full of references to a God whom we might describe as 'triadic' or 'threefold' (Matthew 28:19. 2 Corinthians 13:14. Romans 1:1-4), though it was only much later on that the Christian Church saw the full implications of this truth, and that the doctrine of the Trinity in its most complete sense finally emerged.

The Bible seems to indicate different spheres of activity for each person of the Trinity. God the Father is chiefly associated with the work of creation (Genesis 1:1), God the Son with redemption (Galatians 4:4,5) and God the Holy Spirit, who indwells the Christian believer, with sanctification (Romans 8:11. Ephesians 3:16). But we must not try to draw a hard-and-fast line. There is a good deal of overlapping as, for example, when Jesus is spoken of as indwelling the Christian (Ephesians 3:17) and sharing in the creative work of God the Father (Hebrews 1:2).

When considering this truth, there are certain errors which we must avoid. We must not think on the one hand of a God who

118

simply reveals himself in three different ways, rather like a man who has three separate occupations—father, footballer and fireman. There are three distinct persons, not just one person disguised in three different ways. For example all three were manifested at the baptism of Jesus (Matthew 3:16,17).

On the other hand we must be careful not to separate the persons to such an extent that instead of one God we have three, and think of them as partners in a firm, each responsible for different areas of work, and independent of one another. The presence of one means the presence of all (John 14:16,18,23).

As with so many scriptural mysteries, the truth lies not in the middle, nor at one extreme or the other, but at both extremes at once. There are three distinct and definable persons, and yet there is only one God.

It is because this truth is beyond our comprehension, that human attempts to illustrate it are futile or at best limited. Either we end up with one person revealing himself in three different ways, or with three people who, however united in will and purpose, are not essentially one. Even the analogy of the electric fire (helpful up to a point, with its invisible power, visible light and palpable warmth) really breaks down at this point, because, as every scientist knows, power, light and warmth are simply three manifestations of the same thing, namely energy.

Perhaps a more promising line is to be found in the relationship which exists between thought (God), word (Christ) and breath (the Holy Spirit) (John 1:1,14; 20:22). I sometimes think, too, as I am motoring, of those stretches of road which comprise three distinct routes, for example A3, A272, A325; while the name 'Trinity Oak' is given to those trees which seem to be quite separate and distinct, and yet on closer inspection are seen to stem from the same bole or base. A book, too, may be said to exist in three distinct ways—in the mind of the writer, on the printed page, and in the imagination of the reader.

Truth

1. *The personal meaning.* The word is applied to God as a description of the absolute trustworthiness and reliability of his character. In one place he is actually described as 'the God whose name is Amen' and 'the God of Amen' (Isaiah 65:16 NEB), meaning much the same as we do when we describe someone as 'a man of his word'; while 'the God of truth' (Deuteronomy 32:4) is a

title which is also applied to him. But God's truth is not thought of as something static, for it is a living force which he 'sends forth' (Psalm 57:3) into the world. It is the standard by which he judges mankind (Psalm 96:13), requiring it in the depths of our innermost being (Psalm 51:5).

2. *The doctrinal meaning.* Here, and mainly in the New Testament, the word applies to what is basic and real as opposed to what is merely superficial and false. When Jesus said, 'I am ... the truth' (John 14:6), he meant that he was the one authentic answer to all the problems that have vexed mankind down the ages. 'The truth of the gospel' (Galatians 2:5) means that it provides the one and only way of man's salvation. Jesus is 'the true bread' (John 6:32,35) and 'the true vine' (John 15:1), because he alone is the source of satisfaction and life. And the Holy Spirit will guide the followers of Jesus 'into all the truth' (John 16:13), because he will teach them the difference between good and evil, right and wrong, truth and error.

It is important to remember that truth in the Bible is not just something that we are expected to believe, but something we must obey (Romans 2:8; 10:16). Just as the truth about my physical condition will dictate my diet, exercise and manner of life, so the truth about God will determine how I live, and how he must be obeyed.

U

Unbelief

The Bible never finds any excuse for unbelief. We read that Jesus was 'taken aback' (Mark 6:6 NEB) by the lack of faith he encountered, and it was the principal sin of which he told his disciples that the Holy Spirit would accuse and convict the world (John 16:9).

The reason for this is that unbelief in effect makes God a liar (1 John 5:10), casting doubt on his integrity and character, and therefore amounting to blasphemy. This is why we find the unbelievers or faithless so severely judged (Luke 12:46. Revelation 21:8), along with others whose sins may seem at first sight more blatant and heinous; for 'without faith it is impossible to please God' (Hebrews 11:6).

Unbelief in the Bible is always regarded as tantamount to rebellion, a moral rather than an intellectual problem (Hebrews 3:12). Where there is honest doubt, as in the case of John the Baptist (Luke 7:19-23), or the father of the epileptic boy (Mark 9:24), or Thomas (John 20:24-29), it was always dealt with gently by Jesus, because there was a great desire to believe, and it was the mind and not the will that was at fault. The mind can be enlightened (John 7:17), but the rebellious will has to be broken.

121

Wisdom

1. *The wisdom of God.* God himself, referred to in one place as 'the only wise God' (Romans 16:27), is represented in the Bible as the source and fount of all true wisdom (Job 12:13. Daniel 2:20-23). But his wisdom is not theoretical, it is intensely practical. It is seen in his creative activity in the world (Psalms 104:24; 136:5. Proverbs 3:19). It is seen in his great plan of redemption (Romans 11:33) as revealed in the person of Christ (1 Corinthians 1:24) and broadcast through his Church (Ephesians 3:10).

2. *The wisdom of man.* The Bible makes it very plain that wisdom is one of the most desirable qualities there is. 'For wisdom is better than rubies; and all the things that may be desired are not to be compared to it' (Proverbs 8:11). Indeed, so precious is it felt to be, that it is in many places personified (Proverbs 9:1-6), and true happiness and success in life consist in 'finding wisdom' (Proverbs 3:13).

True spiritual wisdom is not to be confused with the wisdom of this world (James 3:15), which is incapable of knowing or understanding God (1 Corinthians 1:18-25). It is the gift of God himself (1 Chronicles 22:12. 2 Chronicles 1:11,12), and may be sought and found through prayer (James 1:5,6).

Again, it is very practical. 'The fear of the Lord is the beginning of wisdom' (Proverbs 9:10), and the truly wise man in God's sight is the one who knows God's will (Colossians 1:9); who studies, understands and is then able to expound the truths of Scripture (Colossians 3:16; Acts 6:10); and whose daily walk as a Christian is conducted in a sensible manner, 'making the most of the time' (Ephesians 5:15-17). Such wisdom too is not opinionated and contentious, but gracious, peaceable, reasonable and kind (James 3:17).

Witness

In the ordinary way this word was used much as we use it today, to authenticate a signature perhaps, or sometimes in a judicial sense. It illustrates the fact that the Christian must be able to speak from first-hand experience (Acts 1:22; 10:39), give clear evidence of Christ's work in his heart, and stand up to cross-examination, sometimes of an unfriendly sort.

The Greek word for 'witness' is *martus*, from which our word 'martyr' is derived. This translation appears once or twice in the AV (Acts 22:20. Revelation 2:13) and gradually came to be used in common speech to describe a Christian whose faith in Christ had led to his death. In other words, a martyr was a witness who had been 'faithful unto death' (Revelation 2:10).

Although the normal application of this word in the New Testament is to the followers of Jesus and the testimony they are able to give of his love and power, there are occasional instances where it is applied to God himself (Romans 1:9), to the Holy Spirit (Hebrews 10:15. Romans 8:16) and to conscience (Romans 2:15) when they are summoned to support what is being done or said.

Word

There are several different senses in which this word is used in the Bible.

1. It is used to describe the divine edict by which the world was first brought into being, for we read that 'by the word of the Lord were the heavens made' (Psalm 33.6-9).

2. Mainly in the Old Testament it was a special, personal communication from God to man which he in turn was very often required to pass on to others. Frequently we read, for example, that 'the word of the Lord came to' one of his servants (Jeremiah 1:4 &c). When it did so, it had a special authority and urgency, and led to the obvious corollary, 'Thus saith the Lord' (Jeremiah 2:5 AV).

3. One very specialised use occurs in John's writings where Jesus is spoken of as the 'Word' (John 1:1. 1 John 1:1). It is a difficult concept, but it expresses the means whereby a transcendent God can reveal himself to his creatures. The Thought or Wisdom or Idea behind the universe embodies itself in a Word—a meaningful utterance.

4. 'The word' is also frequently used as a synonym of the gospel—a rendering often preferred by the RSV and NEB. We read, for example, of 'the word of his grace' (Acts 20:32), 'the word (message RSV) of salvation' (Acts 13:26 AV), 'the word of reconciliation' (2 Corinthians 5:19) and frequently 'the word of God' (Acts 4:31); and all these phrases are intended to emphasize some important aspect of the gospel.

5. Finally, 'the word' is often used for the written record of God's revelation, or in other words, as much of the Bible as existed at any particular time. In the psalms, particularly in Psalm 119, for example, it frequently occurs, and means the same thing as God's laws, statutes and judgements; while in the New Testament we learn something of its indestructibility (1 Peter 1:24,25), and of the help it can be to the Christian as a sword in his fight against temptation (Ephesians 6:17), as a moral and spiritual looking-glass (James 1:23-25), and as the food to nourish and sustain his Christian life. He is to receive it, study it and obey it (Matthew 4:4).

Works

We find this word used to describe God's creative activity (Psalm 104:24) in the world and his providential power and goodness in history (Psalm 107:8); and also the 'good works' (John 10:32) which Jesus did, as he went about healing, helping and teaching. But it also has a further technical meaning in the New Testament when it is applied to man, for it is made clear that his good works (or 'deeds', as the NEB has it) cannot earn him any merit in the sight of God, and count for nothing so far as his eternal salvation is concerned (Galatians 2:16. Titus 3:5); and indeed they only aggravate his condition, because they engender pride (Ephesians 2:8-10).

On the other hand, while they can never be the cause of man's salvation, they must be one of its most immediate and obvious results. We cannot be saved 'by' good works, but we are saved 'unto' or 'for' them (Ephesians 2:10). They are the fruit by which our Christian profession will be judged, and we are to be 'zealous of

124

good works' (Titus 2:14), to incite others to be the same (Hebrews 10:24) and in this way to glorify God (1 Peter 2:12).

World

Apart from one or two obvious references to the world as the created universe (John 1:10), or the inhabited earth (John 3:16; 16:21), the word 'world' in the New Testament is used to describe the empire of Satan, the 'domain of darkness' (Colossians 1:13 NEB) in contrast to the Kingdom of God.

It is this world which refuses to recognize the creative rights of God over man (1 Corinthians 1:21) or the sovereignty of Christ. It has its own standards, values and principles, the chief hall-marks of which are pride and covetousness (1 John 2:16).

The Christian cannot escape this world (John 17:15), any more than a doctor can escape disease, for then his influence as 'the light of the world' and 'the salt of the earth' (Matthew 5:13-16) would be altogether lost. He is to be in the world, but not of it. He must not love the world (1 John 2:15), or allow himself to be moulded by its standards and attitudes (Romans 12:2). He must be ready for its misunderstanding and hostility (John 15:18), but in the power of Christ and through faith in him he need not be overwhelmed by its influence (John 16:33. 1 John 5:4).

Through his death and resurrection Jesus has overcome the world (John 16:33), defeating 'the prince (or ruler) of this world' (John 16:11), that is to say, Satan himself. Not only therefore is he able to keep his followers 'untarnished by the world' (James 1:27 NEB), but he has passed sentence of death upon it, so that one day it will disappear with all its passions and lusts (1 Corinthians 7:31. 1 John 2:17), and give place to 'new heavens and a new earth wherein dwelleth righteousness' (2 Peter 3:13).

Worship

The root of this word is the kind of service rendered by a slave to his master which is based on reverence, awe and wonder. We see it perhaps in its simplest and most personal form in Genesis 24:26, but as time went on, it became more of a congregational act (1 Chronicles 29:20), and was associated with greater formality and ritual.

In the New Testament we find that Jesus took part in public worship (Luke 4:16), and never criticised it as such; but he saw the dangers of hypocrisy in worship, and warned people against honouring God with their lips while their hearts and minds were

125

far from him (Matthew 15:8). It was 'in spirit and in truth' that he taught people to worship God (John 4:24), not only in outward forms or words.

We learn little from the rest of the New Testament about the future development of public worship. It became particularly associated with the Lord's Day (Acts 20:7), and often took place in quite informal gatherings in the homes of Christians (Colossians 4:15) where 'house-churches' were formed. No doubt singing and praise played an important part (Ephesians 5:19), and there would be readings from God's word (Colossians 3:16), and opportunities for the exercise of spiritual gifts (1 Corinthians 14:26); and perhaps the climax would be the sharing in the love-feast, which was followed by the Lord's Supper (1 Corinthians 11:23-28).